AND YOU WILL BE MY WITNESSES

*31 Devotionals to Encourage
a Spirit of Everyday Evangelism*

Edited by Matt Queen and Alex Sibley

SEMINARY HILL
PRESS

And You Will Be My Witnesses: 31 Devotionals to Encourage a Spirit of Everyday Evangelism
Edited by Matt Queen and Alex Sibley
Copyright © 2019 by Seminary Hill Press

Seminary Hill Press (SHP) is the publishing arm of Southwestern Baptist Theological Seminary, 2001 West Seminary Drive, Fort Worth, Texas 76115.

Layout/design by Caitlyn Jameson.

ISBN-10: 1-7327740-1-3
ISBN-13: 978-1-7327740-1-8

INTRODUCTION

"But you will receive power when the Holy Spirit has come on you, and you will be my witnesses in Jerusalem, in all Judea and Samaria, and to the end of the earth" (Acts 1:8).

Immediately prior to His ascension to the right hand of the throne of God, the resurrected Jesus delivers this charge to His disciples, declaring that they will be His witnesses to the ends of the world. This same charge stands for us today, a charge to declare to the whole world the Gospel of Jesus Christ—a message of repentance for the forgiveness of sins; a pronouncement of the grace of God for the salvation of all who believe by faith; a proclamation of the life, death, resurrection, and ascension of the Son of God on behalf of sinners for the glory of God the Father.

We have been charged to share this message. This task of evangelism has been given to us. *We* will be His witnesses, even to the end of the earth. This book aims to encourage the body of believers in fulfilling this great mission.

Many resources have been written about the how and why of evangelism, but this resource has a different focus. Rather than explore the theology behind the evangelistic task or recommend particular evangelism methods and strategies, this resource focuses on the personal evangelist's heart. While theology and methodology will certainly not be neglected, this book specifically aims to encourage in readers a spirit of everyday evangelism by speaking directly to their hearts through the Word of God.

Designed as a 31-day devotional, this book presents focused expositions of select Scripture passages from the Gospels and Acts pertaining to evangelism. When read along with an open Bible, these devotionals will illuminate the Scripture's teaching on various aspects of the evangelistic task, highlighting how the likes of Paul, Peter, John, Stephen, Philip, John the Baptist, and even Jesus Himself went about proclaiming the message of God's salvation for the world.

The devotionals are intentionally application-focused, and points of guided prayer are also provided in order to facilitate readers' proper response to the Scripture passages studied. Additionally, each devotional contains a particular main idea derived from the Scripture worthy of special contemplation.

All of these elements are combined in order to draw readers into the presence of God as they encounter Him and His teaching through His Word. As they do so, we pray that the Holy Spirit will cultivate within them a heart for the lost, that they would seek to share the Gospel every day, everywhere, with everyone they meet. This is what everyday evangelism looks like, and we believe this is what obedience to Jesus' Acts 1:8 charge looks like. We pray, therefore, that this resource will encourage readers toward that end.

The devotionals that constitute this book are written by faculty, students, and alumni of Southwestern Baptist Theological Seminary. However, though written by scholars, these are not written only for scholars. Rather, they are written in such a way as to be read by scholars and laypersons alike, that all in the body of Christ may be encouraged to proclaim the Gospel to the lost.

So, brothers and sisters, as you begin this month-long journey,

- prepare yourself to see the heart of God revealed through His Word,
- seek to have His compassion and love for the lost,
- glean wisdom and best practices from the early evangelists of the church,
- be encouraged for the evangelistic task,
- and go!

Don't let this encouragement go to waste; don't let this guided study of the Word be for nothing. As you see the heart of God revealed, join Him in His work of seeking and saving the lost. As a witness for Christ, shout from the mountaintops that Jesus Christ is Lord!

Matt Queen and Alex Sibley
Southwestern Baptist Theological Seminary
Fort Worth, Texas

DAY 1

LUKE 3:1-18

Main Idea: *We must call people to genuine repentance as we proclaim the name of Jesus.*

"Prepare the way for the Lord." With these and many other words, John the Baptist prepares the people to receive the coming Messiah. As one of the first New Testament evangelists, John sets an important precedent for the evangelists who are to come, including those of us who proclaim the Messiah today. Specifically, John provides two important foundations for all later evangelism: what we must call people to do, and whom we must preach.

"Produce fruit consistent with repentance." John comes preaching a baptism of repentance for the forgiveness of sins (Luke 3:3). Such repentance, he teaches, must manifest itself outwardly through actions. This is not to say that faith comes by works, but rather that true faith demonstrates itself through works. In short, repentance—a genuine turning away from sin to God—bears fruit (v. 8).

A truly repentant man who has two shirts should share with him who has none; and he who has food should do likewise (v. 11). Repentant tax collectors should collect no more than what they have been ordered to take (v. 13). Repentant soldiers must not take money from anyone by force, or accuse anyone falsely, but should be content with their wages (v. 14). In summary, the people of God should not be recognized as selfish, unloving, deceiving, stealing, extorting, or greedy. Rather, they should love God with all their heart, and with all their soul, and with all their mind; and they should love their neighbors as themselves (Matthew 22:36-40). They are to be recognized by love, joy, peace, patience, kindness, goodness, faithfulness, gentleness, and self-control as the Holy Spirit produces these things within them through their close walk with Him (Galatians 5:22-25).

Brothers and sisters, this teaching is of great importance for us in the evangelistic task. As personal evangelists, we do not call people simply to pray a prayer. We are not offering them "fire insurance" or a "get out of hell free" card that allows them to live however they want and then go to heaven after they die, regardless of whether they truly had a relationship with the Lord. Instead, we are calling people to genuine repentance—a turning away from sin to God. And such repentance ought to be visible; it should manifest itself through actions and heart attitudes.

Some who come to John apparently assume that their Jewish identity is sufficient for their salvation (Luke 3:8). But such is not the case. In a similar way, one cannot say, "I attend church each Sunday; therefore, I am saved," or, "Though I do not walk daily with the Lord, I prayed a prayer when I was younger, and therefore, I will go to heaven when I die." A prayer of salvation does not comprise magic words, and there is nothing inherently salvific about church attendance. While true faith should manifest partially through church attendance, this, in itself, does not save—it is merely outward fruit of an internal reality. This internal reality—that is, salvation—comes about through genuine repentance: turning away from sin and self and the things of this world toward God, and professing Him as Lord. And more than professing, but also *following* Him as Lord. This leads to change in behavior, for the truly repentant no longer follow themselves, but Jesus.

As personal evangelists, this is what we call people to do—follow Jesus. And such following bears visible fruit. Thus, when we evangelize, we do not invite people simply to pray a prayer; we invite them to life transformation.

"One who is more powerful than I am is coming." Many wonder whether John could be the Messiah, but he never allows for any ambiguity on the matter; he clearly proclaims that he is merely a forerunner and nothing more. "I baptize you with water," John declares, "but one who is more powerful than I am is coming. I am not worthy to untie the strap of his sandals. He will baptize you with the Holy Spirit and fire" (v. 16).

Here, John makes two claims about Jesus. First, Jesus has a greater ministry than he, for Jesus will separate the righteous (those who put their faith in Him and are baptized with the Holy Spirit) from the unrighteous (those who reject Him), with the former going to eternal life and the latter to eternal punishment (v. 17; see also Matthew 25:31-46). Second, not only does Jesus have the greater ministry, but Jesus Himself is mightier, and John declares that he is not worthy even to untie Jesus' sandals.

From this second point we derive the next major takeaway for us as personal evangelists. John comes preaching boldly and authoritatively, but still, he does not preach himself. He does not proclaim his own name, nor does he seek his own glory. Instead, he clearly points to One who is yet to come—the Savior Jesus Christ. Indeed, John's entire purpose is to testify to the Light, that all might believe through him (John 1:7-8). He himself says that the reason he came baptizing is that Jesus might be revealed to Israel (1:31). Furthermore, when Jesus does come, John declares, "He must increase, but I must decrease" (3:30). John preaches not himself, but Jesus Christ as Lord.

What great humility John must have possessed! Brothers and sisters, may we seek to cultivate that same humility within ourselves. When we evangelize, may we not seek to exalt ourselves, promote our own name, or obtain any kind of glory. Rather, let us follow John's example and proclaim the precious, saving name of Jesus, for there is no other name under heaven that has been given among men by which we must be saved (Acts 4:12).

"Everyone will see the salvation of God" (Luke 3:6). This Old Testament prophecy pointed to both John's and Jesus' coming, and with the commencement of John's ministry, its fulfillment began. This fulfillment now continues today as believers in the 21st century follow John's example, calling people to genuine repentance—true life transformation—as they proclaim not themselves, but Jesus Christ as Lord. Brothers and sisters, may these two elements serve as the bedrock of our personal evangelism as we continue to spread the message of God's salvation to all mankind.

– Alex Sibley

Guided Prayer:

- Thank the Lord that He has saved you from sin and death, transformed your life, and called you to be a witness for Him.
- Pray that in your evangelism, God will help you to clearly articulate that your listeners must not merely pray a prayer in order to be saved, but rather genuinely repent, turning from sin to God.
- Pray that you will remain humble in your evangelism, promoting not yourself but Jesus. To Him be all the glory!

DAY 2

Main Idea: *Jesus' early preaching provides a model of evangelism for us today, signifying its context, content, and call.*

John the Baptist prepared the way, and now Jesus has come. The baton has been passed from the lesser to the greater, and Jesus Christ Himself now takes center stage. Certainly, Jesus preached much during his time on earth, but Mark here provides for us a helpful summary of Jesus' core message from the beginning: "The time is fulfilled, and the kingdom of God has come near. Repent and believe the good news" (Mark 1:15).

Here, we see three core components of Jesus' evangelism—its context, content, and call. Properly understood, this alliterative trio of components provides a helpful model for us to follow today. Indeed, what better example to follow for our evangelism than Jesus, the source and perfecter of our faith (Hebrews 12:2)? Let's look at each component in turn:

Context for evangelism: "The time is fulfilled." The prophets foresaw these days. Israel eagerly anticipated them. Scripture pointed to their arrival. And now the fullness of time has come. History has reached its climax. The Word has become flesh. And Jesus Christ is revealed, full of grace and truth.

This is the context for Jesus' message. In short, He is here! The Son of God has come! His name—Jesus—means "the Lord saves," and indeed, He has come to save. And more than to save, but *to seek* and to save those who are lost. This glorious Savior has come searching so that the lost may be found.

This is not only the context for Jesus' message, but for ours as well. Jesus has come; He has died on the cross; He has defeated sin and death; He has ascended on high; and from the heavenly throne, He now offers salvation by grace through faith to all who believe. This is the context in which we evangelize. The way of salvation has been gifted to us, and it has come through Jesus. Now, because "the time is fulfilled," we can be saved; we can be made right with God; we can have an abundant, God-filled life now, and then spend eternity with Him in heaven after we die. These glorious truths compel us to evangelize.

Content of evangelism: "The kingdom of God has come near." From Old Testament times, the Israelites assumed the Kingdom of God would be an earthly kingdom, and the Messiah an earthly king. But this was never God's plan. The Kingdom of God is not of this world, but is a heavenly kingdom, and Jesus reigns as King not from a physical throne here on earth, but from the heavenly throne above the universe. At Jesus' coming, the Kingdom of God is said to be near because the King has come to earth and is walking in our midst as the embodiment of that Kingdom. And while here, that King seeks to gather citizens to join Him in his heavenly home.

This is the content of our evangelism. We proclaim Jesus Christ as King and Lord of all. He rules and reigns, and we are subject to Him, whether we choose to be or not (see Psalm 2). As King, He bears authority to judge; and judgment is coming, when the citizens of His Kingdom will be separated from those outside of it—the righteous from the unrighteous. The latter will go away into eternal punishment, but the former into eternal life (Matthew 25:31-46; Luke 3:17).

But to be clear, this gracious King grants us citizenship in heaven if we put our faith in Him—this is what makes one "righteous." Jesus made a way for our salvation. And how did He accomplish such a thing? By dying on a cross in our place. He, our King, paid the penalty of our sin at the price of His own life so that we might be saved. In being saved, we become citizens of His Kingdom, with the promise of eternal life graciously granted to us. This is the message we have heard and believed, and it is the message we must declare to the lost so that they may also be saved.

Call for response in evangelism: "Repent and believe the good news." In light of the context and content of Jesus' evangelism, this third component almost goes without saying. If the lost are saved by repentance and faith, then we must call them to repentance and faith. If they must believe the Gospel in order to be saved, then after we share the Gospel, we must invite them to believe it. The Gospel beckons a response, and so when we evangelize, we must not fail to call for a response. Such is the model that Jesus set forth, and it is imperative that we follow His example, for "everyone *who calls on the name of the Lord* will be saved" (Romans 10:13, emphasis added).

So in your evangelism, follow the model set forth by Jesus— understand the context in which you evangelize, employ the proper content in your message, and then call your hearers to respond. In short, do as Jesus did!

– Alex Sibley

Guided Prayer:

- Thank God for sending Jesus in the fullness of time, that we might be reconciled to Him.
- Pray that God will assist you in understanding and properly articulating the content of the Gospel.
- Pray that God will empower you to be faithful in extending a call to respond each time you evangelize, that everyone who hears the Gospel message may have the opportunity to call on the name of Jesus and be saved.

JOHN 3:1-21

Main Idea: *We must be careful not to get caught up in theological discourses, but rather call unbelievers to be born again.*

Often, when evangelizing, believers find themselves in theological debates with unbelievers. Issues regarding the interpretation of days of creation, the marriage between "the sons of God" and "the daughters of mankind" (Genesis 6:2), the existence of dinosaurs, or some other secondary topic occupy what is supposed to be a witnessing encounter to save a precious soul. If believers successfully address the issue, they may gain confidence in their apologetic prowess. However, in leaving the conversation, they cannot help but think, "Did I even discuss the person's spiritual need of salvation?"

Have you ever been sidetracked in an evangelism encounter? When witnessing, do you spend most of the time addressing issues other than salvation? Or, more importantly, have you tried explaining the person of Jesus without first identifying the individual's need for the Savior? Jesus reminds us in John 3:1-21 that every person has a spiritual need that demands priority in our witnessing encounters.

Consider Nicodemus, "a man from the Pharisees," "a ruler of the Jews," and a "teacher of Israel." Desiring to have a theological discourse, he inquires of Jesus and His miracles. He says to Him, "Rabbi, we know that you are a teacher who has come from God, for no one could perform these signs you do unless God were with him" (v. 2). Nicodemus, representing his religious institution, which specialized in knowing and teaching the law, wonders how Jesus can perform such signs despite not being part of Nicodemus' religious assembly. Ironically, through this theological discourse, Jesus reveals the spiritual ignorance of those like Nicodemus, who think they "know" spiritual matters.

Rather than speak about matters of lesser importance, such as what Nicodemus came to talk about, Jesus cuts straight to Nicodemus' most pressing need—his spiritual need. Jesus says to him, "Truly I tell you, unless someone is born again, he cannot see the kingdom of God" (v. 3).

Perhaps caught off guard, Nicodemus continues his theological inquiry by proposing two questions. First, he asks, "How can anyone be born when he is old? Can he enter his mother's womb a second time and be born?" (v. 4). In reply, Jesus explains that men must be born of the Spirit in order to enter the Kingdom of God. They are not born a second time in a physical sense, but rather spiritually, from above. Jesus clarifies, "Whatever is born of the flesh is flesh, and whatever is born of the Spirit is spirit" (v. 6). Cautioning Nicodemus not to be surprised, Jesus illustrates that the spiritual birth is an unseen reality to the world (vv. 7-8).

Still in disbelief, Nicodemus asks a second question—"How can these things be?" (v. 9). Now, for the third time, Nicodemus evidences his ignorance, which stems from his lack of a second, spiritual birth. Jesus facetiously responds, "Are you a teacher of Israel and don't know these things?" (v. 10). Jesus questions how Nicodemus can serve as a spiritual leader to others yet fail to understand how one enters God's Kingdom. Contrastively, Jesus reveals His ability to speak confidently on these things as the One who "has ascended into heaven" and "descended from heaven"—that is, "the Son of Man" (v. 13). He explains "how these things can be": one becomes born again by believing in the crucifixion of the Son of Man on the cross (v. 15).

Jesus continues with one of the most well-known verses in Scripture, followed by perhaps one of the most neglected verses in Scripture, but one that is no less beautiful. First, He says, "For God loved the world in this way: He gave his one and only Son, so that everyone who believes in him will not perish but have eternal life" (v. 16). Then, He explains, "For God did not send his Son into the world to condemn the world, but to save the world through him" (v. 17). This is the Gospel message—God so loved the world that He sent Jesus to save it. And these beautiful verses come about in response to Nicodemus' inquiry about Jesus' miracles. Clearly, Jesus does not allow Himself to be distracted from the goal of this and every witnessing encounter—that is, the salvation of a precious soul.

Jesus' encounter with Nicodemus reminds us that evangelism aims to call sinners to believe in Christ and what He did on the cross. Jesus elaborates in the verses that follow that as a result of the new birth, the believer does not experience judgment (v. 18a). He practices truth, having been born a second time, from above, by God (v. 21). Sadly, however, the one who does not believe has been judged already because he loves darkness and his sinful deeds (vv. 18b-20).

All of us at some point encounter a Nicodemus, one who knows theological topics of the Bible or religion but does not know of his spiritual need for salvation. What will be your response? Will you offer him an apologetic debate? Will you seek to answer every question regarding his theological inquiry? Or will you follow Jesus' example, remembering that these individuals don't need more theological discourse? As with Nicodemus, such people have not been born again because of their unbelief (v. 11). Therefore, their greatest need is for you to do as Jesus did—to tell them the Gospel and invite them to believe in the Gospel, so that they may accept the Gospel and become born again. For then, they "will not perish but have eternal life" (v. 16).

- Carl J. Bradford

Guided Prayer:

- Thank God for sending His Son to save the world so that we might not perish, but have eternal life.
- Pray that in your witnessing encounters, you will not get caught up in theological discourses, but rather remember your listeners' greatest need—to be born again.

- Pray that as you share the Gospel with unbelievers, they will set their theological questions aside and focus instead on the beautiful Gospel message, choosing Light and eternal life rather than darkness, evil, and condemnation.

DAY 4

JOHN 4:1-26

Main Idea: *We must seek others cross-culturally.*

When Christians hear the word "evangelism," they tend to think of sharing the Gospel with those who live in a similar context as they do. However, the Great Commission of Jesus instructs us to "make disciples of all nations" (Matthew 28:19). Despite the commission of Jesus, until recent decades, only those formally called "missionaries" have evangelized people of other cultures. Why the lack of engaging those of different cultures?

One reason is that recognized missiologists have historically asserted that cross-cultural evangelism cannot occur unless one adopts the foreign culture and builds long-term relationships. Additionally, they contend that cross-cultural evangelism is done best without words. Cross-cultural evangelism, in this conception, thus requires a long-term commitment and a great expenditure of effort.

But is this assessment accurate? Arguably, no. While learning the culture of potential converts and building relationships certainly help the personal evangelist better understand another's lifestyle, they do not ensure successful evangelism of that person. Furthermore, the notion of sharing the Gospel "without words" is extremely dangerous.

What, then, should be a believer's method of cross-cultural evangelism? A look at Jesus' encounter with the Samaritan woman will help us develop a personal method for cross-cultural evangelism, one that aligns with Jesus' Great Commission and leaves out much of what the supposed expert missiologists have suggested.

Having left Judea for Galilee, Jesus "had to travel through Samaria" because of the divine cross-cultural appointment that awaited Him (John 4:3-4). Jesus, wearied from His journey and sitting by a well, asks for a drink of water from a Samaritan woman (vv. 6-7). Surprised that Jesus would engage her, the woman replies, "How is it that you, a Jew, ask for a drink from me, a Samaritan woman?" (v. 9). Determined to engage the woman in evangelism, Jesus answers, "If you knew the gift of God, and who is saying to you, 'Give me a drink,' you would ask him, and he would give you living water" (v. 10). Perplexed, the woman questions Jesus' ability to provide such water (vv. 11-12). Afterward, the remainder of the encounter proceeds in this way:

> Jesus said, "Everyone who drinks from this water will get thirsty again. But whoever drinks from the water that I will give him will never get thirsty again. In fact, the water I will give him will become a well of water springing up in him for eternal life."
>
> "Sir," the woman said to him, "give me this water so that I won't get thirsty and come here to draw water." "Go call your husband," he told her, "and come back here." "I don't have a husband," she answered. "You have correctly said, 'I don't have a husband,'" Jesus said. "For you've had five husbands, and the man you now have is not your husband. What you have said is true." "Sir," the woman replied, "I see that you are a prophet. Our fathers worshiped on this mountain, but you Jews say that the place to worship is in Jerusalem."
>
> Jesus told her, "Believe me, woman, an hour is coming when you will worship the Father neither on this mountain nor in Jerusalem. You Samaritans worship what you do not know. We worship what we do know, because salvation is from the Jews. But an hour is coming, and is now here, when the true worshipers will worship the Father in Spirit and in truth. Yes, the Father wants such people to

worship him. God is spirit, and those who worship him must worship in Spirit and in truth." The woman said to him, "I know that the Messiah is coming" (who is called Christ). "When he comes, he will explain everything to us." Jesus told her, "I, the one speaking to you, am he" (vv. 13-26).

Jesus' participation in cross-cultural evangelism not only leads this woman to salvation, but many others as well—"Now many Samaritans from that town believed in him because of what the woman said when she testified, 'He told me everything I ever did'" (v. 39). Why is Jesus' evangelism so successful? Does He adopt the Samaritans' culture? Does He wait for multiple encounters?

Notice Jesus' method of evangelism to the Samaritan woman. First, **He engages her**. In doing so, he crosses many taboo and sociocultural barriers of the day. Jesus converses in public with a woman, one who has been with multiple men, not to mention the fact that she is a Samaritan, whom the "Jews do not associate with" (v. 9). Additionally, He is willing to drink from her water pot, which would have been deemed unclean.

Second, **He identifies the woman's spiritual need for salvation**. Unlike some today, Jesus does not seek to meet a physical need of the woman or build a long-term relationship before engaging her spiritually (and He certainly does not try to evangelize without words). Instead, He utilizes their *first* encounter as an opportunity to speak of salvation (vv. 13-14) and to confront unapologetically her sinful lifestyle (vv. 16-18).

Third, **He deals with the woman's misunderstanding of worshiping God** (vv. 20-24). Refusing the attraction of a debate regarding cultural differences, Jesus places greater emphasis on true spiritual worship. So often, believers fight over theological differences yet forget to consider what the Word of God says on the matter.

Last, **He leads the woman to the Messiah—that is, Himself** (v. 26). Jesus gives the woman the only thing that can change her situation. He demonstrates the purpose of all evangelism encounters: presenting Jesus as Savior.

Do you have a personal method of evangelism to engage those of other cultures? Many Christians do not participate in cross-cultural evangelism because they are not sure how to engage the person. Are you one who avoids cross-cultural evangelism at any cost because you don't know how? Do you believe others' culture must be studied and adopted before you can evangelize them successfully?

Thankfully, today, you and I have opportunities to engage unbelievers through cross-cultural evangelism not just through international mission trips, but within our own neighborhoods. And not only do we have opportunities, but we have a method for how to do so, as well, and this method comes from Jesus Christ Himself. So let us follow His example and engage in cross-cultural evangelism, offering living water to people from every nation.

– Carl J. Bradford

Guided Prayer:

- Thank God that, from the time of Jesus, the Gospel has crossed innumerable cultural boundaries, reaching even to your culture so that you could be saved.
- Pray that God will grant you wisdom in how to employ Jesus' method for engaging in cross-cultural evangelism.
- Ask God for boldness in crossing cultural boundaries, that all may hear the Good News of Christ—His offer of living water and eternal life.

DAY 5

--------- **JOHN 4:28-30, 39-42** ---------

Main Idea: *A personal relationship with Christ should drive us to use our story to proclaim His Gospel.*

John 4 recounts one of the more well-known stories in the New Testament. Jesus, in His mercy, proclaims the Good News of His Gospel to a Samaritan woman of ill repute. This story in and of itself is rife with examples from Jesus. In this passage, we see the mercy and grace of Jesus as He ministers to a woman whom many would have hated and neglected; we see the wisdom of Jesus as He uses physical water and the burdens of the past to show this woman her need for His Gospel; and we see the patience of Jesus as He once again explains the purpose of His coming to His disciples. The examples from Jesus in this passage are many, but the woman (yes, that woman) also serves as an example to everyone of how to effectively engage others with the Gospel of Jesus Christ.

John 4:28-29 recounts the immediate action of the woman after trusting in Christ. John writes, "Then the woman left her water jar, went into town, and told the people, 'Come, see a man who told me everything I ever did.'" The response of the woman is to leave behind the weight of the water jar and run and tell others of the power of Jesus. In John 4:14, Jesus says to the woman that "whoever drinks from the water that I will give him will never get thirsty again. In fact, the water I will give him will become a well of water springing up in him for eternal life." The moment this woman trusts in Jesus, she leaves the earthly water behind and runs to tell others of the living water that she has received. The cup of her salvation runs over into her bringing those around her to Jesus.

The woman serves as an example of the **passion** that should fuel evangelism. The encounter she has with Jesus leads her to proclaim His coming to the people around her. Much like the disciples in the book of Acts, this woman cannot help but speak of what she has seen and heard. The passion that fuels her sharing is her own personal experience with Jesus. This is the same passion that must fuel all believers as they set out to proclaim the Gospel of Jesus Christ. Without a personal relationship with Christ, the believer has nothing to proclaim; but with a relationship with Christ, he can proclaim "the immeasurable riches of his grace [displayed] through his kindness to us in Christ Jesus" (Ephesians 2:7).

The woman also serves as an example of the **power** of using a personal testimony in evangelism. Citing her own personal interaction with Jesus, she tells of what Jesus has told her about her past. This woman's personal experience with Jesus serves as a bridge to bring others to Christ Jesus. Just as the woman uses her encounter with Jesus as a tool for sharing about Him, so can today's believer. One of the most powerful tools that all believers have for sharing their faith is their own personal testimony of what Christ has done for them.

When the woman brings the people to Jesus, they find living water for themselves. John 4:42 records the testimony of these new believers: "We no longer believe because of what you said, since we have heard for ourselves and know that this really is the Savior of the world." The response of these individuals shows us another example that the woman provides for us: the **purpose** of a personal testimony is to point people to Jesus. When believers share their testimony, it is easy to make themselves the central point of the story. But the reality is that Jesus is the focal point of our salvation experience, and it is He and He alone who has the power to save. The purpose of a personal testimony is to laud the saving mercies and graces of the Lord Jesus Christ. As believers proclaim their testimonies, the person of Christ and the words of Scripture should be lauded above personal details. The purpose of a testimony is to share the person of Christ and to see others' hearts and lives transformed by Him.

In John 4, readers encounter an unlikely example of a personal evangelist: a woman of ill repute. Yet, because of her response to Christ and faithful witness, she stands as an example to every believer of the passion that fuels evangelism, the power of a personal testimony, and the purpose of a personal testimony. Because of her personal experience with Christ, this woman uses her personal story to point people to the Savior. The joy of her salvation combined with the power of her personal story allows her to show others the person of Jesus. Brothers and sisters, may the joy of our salvation lead us to be bold in sharing our story of Jesus, and may we point all whom we encounter to Jesus Christ.

– Garrison Griffith

Guided Prayer:

- Thank the Lord that, though you are as much a sinner as the Samaritan woman, He showed you mercy and grace and gave you a story to tell of His lovingkindness.
- Pray that you will have the same passion as the Samaritan woman to tell those around you about the saving grace of Jesus.
- Pray that God will help you to use your story to point others to Jesus, and that through your story, others would come to know Him as their Savior.

DAY 6

JOHN 9:1-41

Main Idea: *Our eyes have been opened to the truth of who Jesus is.*

Among the more interesting characters in the Bible is the man born blind in John 9, not the least because, despite being a regular "man on the street," he is able to stand his ground against the more educated Pharisees. That he does so with such humor certainly strengthens his reputation.

Jesus' opening the eyes of this man who has been blind since birth—on a Sabbath, no less—causes no small amount of controversy, and the Pharisees insist on getting the true story. Despite validating the details of Jesus' miracle with multiple sources, they still do not believe. When they force the man to testify for the *third* time in this passage, he notes that they have already heard his story, then asks, "You don't want to become his disciples too, do you?" (v. 27). In other words, he facetiously tells the Pharisees, "You seem awfully interested in this Jesus. If I didn't know better, I'd say you want to abandon your Pharisaical traditions and follow Him, perhaps because, deep down, you want to violate the Sabbath too." Appropriately, the Pharisees respond with childish indignation—"You're that man's disciple, but we're Moses' disciples. We know that God has spoken to Moses. But this man—we don't know where he's from" (vv. 28-29).

Again, the man born blind responds facetiously—"This is an amazing thing! You don't know where he is from, and yet he opened my eyes" (v. 30). The man is sarcastically pointing out that the Pharisees' argument makes no sense—that they do not know where Jesus comes from has no bearing on the fact that Jesus opened his eyes. Thus, after acknowledging their point, the man immediately tosses it aside as the non sequitur that it is and moves on to the matter at hand.

He then reveals a unique insight into the situation that the Pharisees apparently lack. He rightly notes that opening the eyes of a man born blind is an unprecedented miracle, unheard of "throughout history." He profoundly concludes, "If this man were not from God, he wouldn't be able to do anything" (v. 33). Here, we see that the man born blind—previously regarded as either a sinner punished with blindness or the child of sinners who was thus shamed by association—*this* man, and not the more educated Pharisees, is able to see that Jesus is from God. Unable to comprehend this great truth themselves, the Pharisees respond with their usual puerility, "You were born entirely in sin, and are you trying to teach us?" and they throw him out of the synagogue (v. 34).

Later on, Jesus comes to him and affirms that He is "the Son of Man" (vv. 35-37). In response, the man born blind believes, and he worships the Lord.

Though much can be gleaned from this story, Jesus reveals the ultimate point in verse 39—"I came into this world for judgment, in order that those who do not see will see and those who do see will become blind." In other words, when the eyes of the man born blind are opened, he can see, both literally and figuratively, while the Pharisees, who through their knowledge and tradition think they can see, are revealed to be spiritually blind. Thus, God grants insight to a "sinner" and exposes the "righteous" for what they really are—"whitewashed tombs, which appear beautiful on the outside, but inside are full of the bones of the dead and every kind of impurity" (Matthew 23:27).

Brothers and sisters, here is the application of this great passage for us: *We* are the ones who see. *Our* eyes have been opened. God has granted *us* insight so that we can join the man born blind in declaring that Jesus is the Son of God.

And how does that impact our evangelism? We know the truth. We know who Jesus is. Let us, therefore, be confident, and may that confidence manifest through boldness. May we be like the man born blind, who, like us, experienced the miraculous work of Jesus and confidently stands his ground in the face of opposition. And may we, like him, boldly proclaim the truth that our eyes have been opened to see—that Jesus is the Christ.

Those who question us may be intimidating, and they may threaten us and perhaps even our families (see vv. 18-23), but we need not fear, for we have the truth; they are the ones who lack it. We have a sure and solid foundation; their beliefs are baseless and will ultimately collapse. We have the stronger position; therefore, we need not be intimidated.

And all the more so because, when we face them, God, through His Spirit, will grant us the words to say, much as the man born blind is able to stand up to the Pharisees and hold his own against them. So we, too, can trust that when we are challenged, God will grant us insight, and we need only speak the truth that God has entrusted to us. And even if we are "thrown out of the synagogue," Jesus will remain with us, just as He ministers to the man born blind. That is the beauty of our Savior—He opens our eyes, He makes known to us the truth of who He is, and He ministers to us when we need Him. What a glorious Savior.

The man born blind is much like us—a simple "man on the street." And yet he stands his ground, holding fast to the truth, and puts the Pharisees in their place. Though the Pharisees ultimately throw him out of the synagogue, the man born blind wins their verbal sparring match. He is right. He can see. As those whose eyes have also been opened, may we confidently stand our ground as well, boldly proclaiming the truth that God has opened our eyes to see, so that the world may know that Jesus is the Son of God.

– Alex Sibley

Guided Prayer:

- Thank God for opening your eyes to the truth of who He is.

- Ask God for boldness to stand your ground and proclaim the truth that He has entrusted to you.
- Thank God for being the God of all comfort, especially when we are "thrown out of the synagogue."

DAY 7

Main Idea: *We do not need to know the answer to every question; our testimony of Jesus' saving power is enough.*

Though the overall point of this passage was explored in the previous devotional, there is at least one aspect of the man born blind's story still worth examining. When the Pharisees confront him about Jesus' miraculously opening his eyes, they question him about Jesus' character, asserting that He is a sinner. The man born blind replies, "Whether or not he's a sinner, I don't know. One thing I do know: I was blind, and now I can see" (John 9:25).

When we attempt to share the Gospel with unbelievers, we will face questions. More specifically, we will face questions about Jesus and the Bible and God the Father that perhaps we are unable to answer in the moment. Perhaps such questions will even bring to light some of our own personal questions and doubts. "What did Jesus mean when He said that we must hate our families in order to be His disciples (Luke 14:26)?" "Does the Bible really say that homosexuality is a sin, and if so, is that merely a culturally specific and therefore outdated teaching?" "And just how did Noah fit all the animals on the ark?"

But in the midst of evangelism, such questions are largely irrelevant and often signify attempts by unbelievers to dodge the larger issues, issues like sin, judgment, and hell. When confronted with the undeniable reality of their own sin, for example, these unbelievers subvert the issue by lodging a question against the person evangelizing them, hoping to distract from the matter at hand. Similarly, when the Pharisees are confronted with the undeniable reality of Jesus' miraculous work, they stubbornly maintain their position that He is a sinner, and that the man born blind must be lying about his testimony.

The man born blind's response is instructive for us. When faced with the question of the source of Jesus' power—in short, the question of Jesus' deity—the man born blind admits his ignorance of the matter; he cannot answer the question. But rather than become discouraged by his inability to directly quash the Pharisees' attack, he does what he is able to do. He may not know the answer to the question of Jesus' deity, but one thing he does know, and that, he declares—that though he was blind, now he can see.

The man born blind does not know everything there is to know about Jesus. In fact, he knows very little. But he does know something important: Jesus opened his eyes; he has experienced Jesus' miraculous work. This is his testimony. And this, he proclaims. He cannot answer the Pharisees' questions, but he can share what he knows, and in so doing, he proves himself a faithful witness for the Lord.

We will face questions in the midst of our evangelism, and some if not most of these questions will be difficult if not impossible for us to answer in the moment. But we need not become discouraged by our inability to directly quash the attacks that come our way; all we need to do is share what we do know—that Jesus saved us. The Son of God died on a cross for our sins so that we could be forgiven. Then He arose, He ascended to the right hand of the throne of God, and He is coming again. By faith in Him, we have been saved. This, we know. And that is enough for the evangelistic task.

So, brothers and sisters, you will face opposition; you will face questions that you cannot answer. But do not be discouraged, and do not shrink back from the task. For if you have experienced the miraculous work of the Savior Jesus Christ, then you have a story to tell.

So when unbelievers try to distract you with difficult non sequiturs, brush them aside and declare what you know—that Jesus performed a miracle in your life, and now you will never be the same. One day, like the man born blind, you met Jesus, and He changed your life forever. You were spiritually blind, but He opened your eyes to see. You were spiritually dead, but He breathed new life into your bones. And now you walk daily with the ruling, reigning, and soon-returning King of the universe.

By no means should we overlook the fact that the questions that get lodged against us do need to be answered. We should be diligent in our study of God's Word in order to learn all that we can so that we can answer every question, so that no barrier will stand in the way of our evangelism; so that no barrier will stand in the way of an unbeliever coming to faith in Christ.[1]

But let us not count ourselves inadequate if we are confronted by a difficult question to which we do not know the answer. Instead, in such a situation, let us commit to find an answer at a later time, then return to the matter at hand by sharing what we do know—that we were dead, but now, because of Jesus, we are alive. Ultimately in our evangelism, that is enough.

– Alex Sibley

Guided Prayer:

- Thank the Lord Jesus for performing a miracle in your life, saving you from death and graciously granting you eternal life.

---

[1] Consider some brief possible responses to the three questions listed above:

(1) When Jesus told us to hate our families in order to be His disciples, He was speaking of the level of devotion required to follow Him. We should love our families (Matthew 22:39), but we should love Jesus more (Matthew 22:37). In fact, we should love Him so much that our love for our families looks like hate by comparison. *That* is the level of devotion that He requires.

(2) Yes, the Bible does say that homosexuality is a sin (see, for example, 1 Corinthians 6:9-11), and no, it is not a culture-specific command that no longer applies today; it remains an authoritative, God-inspired teaching. Some may find this difficult to accept, but we must submit to God's lordship.

(3) Finally, I honestly don't know how Noah fit all the animals on the ark. But I do believe that the God who created the universe could make a way for that to be possible.

- Pray that God will equip you to share your testimony in such a way that unbelievers' doubts and questions will be cast aside as they see the beauty of the Savior through your story.
- Commit to the Lord that you will diligently study His Word in order to know it well and answer the questions that come your way.

DAY 8

ACTS 2:1-41

Main Idea: *The pouring out of the Holy Spirit on the day of Pentecost initiated our mission to evangelize the world.*

Hundreds of years before Christ, God promised to Israel, through the prophets of old, that He would make a new covenant with them that was unlike the one with Moses. In the new covenant, God would not merely write the law on tablets of stone. Such stones were exterior to the person of faith and were not part of a person's very being. In the new covenant, however, God would write His righteous decrees inside each person of faith—that is, on his heart.

Each person, by nature, then, would live in obedience before God because the righteous ordinances of God would be a part of who he is. Faithfulness, holiness, love, compassion, mercy, truth, justice, generosity, and every other virtue would be internalized. The various qualities of righteousness would simply be part of who a person of faith is by nature.

Included as a blessing of the new covenant was the One who would write this law on their hearts and who would also convey to them forgiveness of sins: the third person of the Holy Trinity, the Holy Spirit. And, furthermore, as a blessing of the new covenant, the faithful of Israel would be taken from their graves, raised bodily from the dead. When the new covenant was completely fulfilled, the people of God would be resurrected, and the Holy Spirit would complete within them, dynamically, the writing of the whole law on their hearts, and they would experience fully all the benefits of being cleansed of their sins (Jeremiah 31:31-34; Ezekiel 36:24-27; 37:1-14).

Finally, after all those years of waiting, God the Father, through the redemptive work of God the Son and by the sanctifying work of God the Spirit, would recreate the Israelites of faith through rebirth. They would be remade inside out; raised from the dust and given new hearts. Completely, not just partially, in body and soul, they would be newly created.

Acts 2:1-41 is all about the inauguration of the new covenant. In a two-part sermon on three different Old Testament texts, Peter proclaims that on the day of Pentecost and in the resurrection of Jesus, God is doing and has recently done new things in fulfillment of promises made long ago. The Old Testament promised that in the last days, the days leading up to the final judgment and the inauguration and completion of blessing, the Lord would do astounding things.

When the twelve apostles, now with the addition of Matthias (1:26), are gathered together and are "all filled with the Holy Spirit" and begin to "speak in different tongues, as the Spirit enable[s] them" (2:4), they experience a fulfillment of the promise of Jesus in Acts 1:8: "you will receive power when the Holy Spirit has come on you, and you will be my witnesses in Jerusalem, in all Judea and Samaria, and to the end of the earth." How amazing that must have been! Jews and Jewish converts from the world over hear the twelve speaking of God's mighty deeds in their own language. Wow.

The apostles are now equipped with the supernatural ability to proclaim the Gospel to the remotest of people in their own language, and Peter jumps at the opportunity. He preaches in the first part of his sermon that this empowerment for Gospel mission is an astounding, inaugural fulfillment of a last-days, new-covenant prophecy. His text is Joel 2:28-32. The phenomenon that is occurring on that day at Pentecost and that will continue in the Spirit-empowered ministry of the apostles as prophesied by Jesus (Acts 1:8) is an authentic but partial fulfillment of Old Testament prophecy concerning the last days. These men are not drunk with wine, but have received from the resurrected, ascended Christ the Spirit, whom He has poured out upon them. They are now supernaturally prophesying and proclaiming the mighty deeds of God in such a way that all Jews and converts present at this time hear the twelve in their own tongue (Acts 2:4, 11b, 17-18, 32-33).

Part two of Peter's sermon is an interpretation and application of Psalm 16:8-11 and 110:1. The first text also points us back to new covenant promises. Recall that they included the blessing of bodily resurrection. Well, before others can be raised, Christ must be raised (1 Corinthians 15:12-23). Peter, preaching in the fullness of the Spirit, proclaims that Psalm 16, written by David, is a prophecy of the resurrection of Christ (Acts 2:22-32), and that Psalm 110 prophesies His ascension to the Father's right hand (vv. 33-35). Together, the psalms teach that the Jesus who was crucified is now the risen, exalted Lord (v. 36)! The last days have dawned.

The personal evangelist finds much to glean from this passage of Scripture. Peter provides a model evangelistic sermon; the fulfillment of prophecies points to a God who keeps His word, including His promise of eternal life to those who believe in Him by faith; the Holy Spirit empowers the witness of the faithful; Spirit-empowered evangelism can produce many converts—the list goes on. But for our purposes, perhaps the most important point of this passage is the fact that the last times have begun, and this provides the context in which we continue to evangelize today. Jesus has been resurrected, the Holy Spirit has been poured out upon believers, and we have been appointed witnesses to proclaim this resurrected Christ in the power of the Spirit to all nations.

And the work remains undone. It is important to note that neither Joel's prophecy nor Psalm 110:1 are entirely fulfilled on the day of Pentecost. Prophecy is frequently fulfilled only partially or in phases until the final day of consummation comes. What we see at this point during Pentecost is God pouring out the Holy Spirit on the twelve apostles, and then about 3,000 others receiving the gift of the Spirit. Not all men and women are so blessed; and only the twelve, not all, are prophesying and proclaiming the mighty deeds of God in a universally understood manner. There is no "blood and fire and a cloud of smoke," no wonders in the sky, the sun does not turn dark, nor the moon to blood, and the passage reports no dreams or visions. There is, however, a mighty noise from heaven along with "tongues like flames of fire," and "many wonders and signs [are] performed through the apostles" (vv. 3, 43). And, all who call on the name of the Lord Jesus Christ that day are saved (vv. 37-41). As to Christ's lordship over all His enemies (Psalm 110:1), the New Testament explains that though this is substantial, God has chosen not to exercise His complete power over His foes just yet. Death and the devil still must be utterly vanquished (1 Corinthians 15:25-28; Hebrews 2:5-8; 10:13; Revelation 20:10).

The remarkable day of Pentecost with its signs and wonders puts the world on notice. The last days have begun. The apostolic preaching is from God the Holy Spirit. Christ is Lord. The gifts of forgiveness of sins and the Holy Spirit are available to all who call upon the name of Jesus. Let us proclaim this name to every corner of the world until all these prophecies are fulfilled and the last days reach their end.

– D. Jeffrey Bingham

Guided Prayer:

- Thank God for pouring out His Spirit upon you, that He may be with you wherever you go and empower your witness to unbelievers.
- Pray that God will help you remain faithful to the evangelistic task until the last days are completed.
- Thank God for the awesome privilege of carrying the name of His Son to the ends of the earth in the power of His Spirit.

DAY 9

ACTS 2:42-47

Main Idea: *To see growth in our evangelistic effectiveness, we must be committed.*

Since it began in the 1960s, Evangelism Explosion has been a popular evangelistic ministry tool used by churches throughout the country. Long before this strategy was ever executed, the early church saw an explosion of evangelism. In Acts 2, Luke recounts this explosion: "Every day the Lord added to their number those who were being saved" (v. 47). How does the early church see such explosive growth? The answer is simple: The church is committed.

Five specific commitments mark the early church as recorded in Acts 2. First, the early church is committed to **discipleship**. Verse 42 indicates that the early believers devote themselves to the apostles' teaching. Based on Matthew 28:19-20, we can assume that the apostles are teaching them to observe all that Jesus commanded them so that the early church members will become true disciples of Christ. The people in the early church devote themselves to this teaching continually as they commit themselves to becoming disciples.

Second, the early church is committed to **fellowship**. Verse 42 also indicates that they devote themselves to fellowship and to the breaking of bread with one another. Verse 44 says that they are together and have all things in common. Verse 46 adds that they are in the temple and sharing meals together day by day. Clearly, the early church members are committed to fellowship with one another. The power of the Gospel and the commitment to grow in Christ supersede whatever previous obligations they may have had or differences they may have exhibited and bring everyone together as they share everything in common.

Third, the early church is committed to **prayer**. Verse 42 concludes by saying that just as the early church is committed to the apostles' teaching and to fellowship, they are also committed to prayer. As verse 43 begins, it says that all of these believers are marked with a sense of awe. As they pray, both corporately and individually, their hearts and spirits are marked with a sense of awe at the work of the Lord.

Fourth, the early church is committed to **stewardship**. Verses 44-45 reveal that the members of the church give of their possessions as any have need and have everything in common. The pattern presented in this text is that when a need arises in one part of the body of Christ, it is answered by another. Ephesians 4:16 illustrates this point, stating in reference to Christ, "From him the whole body, fitted and knit together by every supporting ligament, promotes the growth of the body for building up itself in love by the proper working of each individual part." The individual members of the body help build it up in love by being good stewards of two areas of their lives: their possessions and their talents.

Lastly, the early church is committed to **ambassadorship**. Verses 46-47 note that the church continues to meet in the temple day by day, and the Lord adds to their number daily those who are being saved. At the temple, the early church finds assembled crowds before whom they can bear witness to what Christ has done in their hearts and lives. The message of the early church penetrates the hearts of people each and every day. They serve as ambassadors for the message of Christ. The Apostle Paul later writes in 2 Corinthians 5:20, "Therefore, we are ambassadors for Christ, since God is making his appeal through us." Ambassadors for Christ is exactly what the early church members are to those who are in the temple.

If churches and church members in our day want to see an "evangelism explosion" like that in the early church, the commitments that characterize the early church must characterize believers individually and churches corporately. To truly see an explosion of evangelism in our day, believers must be committed to becoming disciples of Jesus Christ by submitting themselves daily to His commands and regularly submitting themselves to instruction in righteousness.

Believers must also be committed to fellowship with one another. Hebrews 10:25 reminds believers to not neglect "to gather together, as some are in the habit of doing," but to encourage one another, "and all the more as you see the day approaching." Gathering together as God's people is imperative to evangelistic effectiveness, because it is here that we find encouragement for the Great Commission task at hand.

Believers must be committed to prayer with and for one another. In Ephesians 6:18-19, the Apostle Paul reminds his readers to "pray at all times in the Spirit with every prayer and request, and stay alert with all perseverance and intercession for all the saints. Pray also for me, that the message may be given to me when I open my mouth to make known with boldness the mystery of the gospel." Paul's encouragement is not just to pray for each other's needs, but to pray boldly for the advance of the Gospel. It is as we pray for the advance of the Gospel and for the work of God that awe grows in our hearts as we await the Lord's movement.

Believers must also be committed to the faithful stewardship of what God has given them. Those who steward faithfully will give generously to the needs of others and to the work of God through their local church. Generous giving serves as a testimony of God's provision for His people to those within and those outside the church.

Believers must be committed to ambassadorship. Making an appeal for the Gospel to those who are lost is the mission of every member of the body of Christ. Believers must realize that they are all ambassadors for Christ everywhere they go, day by day. Just as the early church takes the message of Christ to the temple day by day, so should believers today take the message into all arenas of life, wherever they find themselves, day by day.

The early church was effective in its mission because it was committed to discipleship, fellowship, prayer, stewardship, and ambassadorship. If we hope to see the Lord move mightily in our day, we must commit ourselves to the same things. If you are looking for somewhere to start today, start with a commitment to prayer. Ask the Lord to advance His Gospel through you and through the believers with whom you worship each and every week. As the awe of what the Lord can do grows in your heart through prayer, may your mouth speak boldly to all who cross your path of this Jesus whom God has raised from the dead, of which we are all witnesses (Acts 2:32).

– Garrison Griffith

Guided Prayer:

- Thank God for saving the lost and adding them to our number.
- Pray that the commitments that characterized the early church would characterize you individually and your church corporately, that you might see an explosion of evangelism.
- Pray that you and your church would maintain a sense of awe at the great wonders that God has performed.

DAY 10

———————— **ACTS 4:1-22** ————————

Main Idea: *Those who spend time with Jesus spend time telling others about Jesus.*

Instead of seeking after the lost, numerous believers spend time searching for the confidence to evangelize.[2] They tell themselves, "If only I had more confidence, I would share the Gospel with my friends and acquaintances who I know need Christ." Imagine how much confidence they think they would need to share Christ with someone who is hostile to the Gospel!

In the middle of the last century, a rodeo clown and steer wrestler named Ken Boen lived in Fort Smith, Arkansas. Boen was hostile to the Gospel and had a reputation in the area as the last person in the world who would ever receive Christ. A number of pastors, evangelists, and lay people attempted to share the Gospel with him, and he invariably rejected their offers to receive Christ. In fact, almost no believer in Fort Smith had any confidence when it came to evangelizing Boen because of the hardness of his heart.

Have you ever been in need of evangelistic confidence? Every believer, at some time or another, has needed evangelistic confidence. One way personal evangelists have found confidence over the years has been to enroll in evangelism training. Evangelism training often provides willing evangelists confidence by teaching them a Gospel script that they can memorize, so they can know what to say when they evangelize.

---

[2] This day's devotional is adapted from chapter 6 of *Everyday Evangelism*, titled "Finding Evangelistic Confidence" (Matt Queen, *Everyday Evangelism* [Fort Worth, Texas: Seminary Hill Press, 2015], 41-43).

While evangelism training does provide willing evangelists with some confidence to know what to say, it does not necessarily always give them confidence to begin evangelistic conversations. How, then, do evangelists find the confidence to share the Gospel with those who are open to hear it as well as with those who are hostile against it? Consider the evangelistic confidence of Peter and John as recorded in Acts 4:13-20.

After healing a lame man in the name of Jesus (3:1-10), Peter and John preach the resurrection from the dead through Jesus in Jerusalem (3:11-26; 4:1-2). The priests, the captain of the temple guard, and the Sadducees take offense and arrest them (4:1-3). Nevertheless, 5,000 of those who hear their message believe in Jesus (v. 4).

The next day, the apostles are put on trial and asked by their accusers, "By what power or in what name have you done this?" (vv. 5-7). With complete confidence and filled with the Holy Spirit, Peter responds that they have done this in the name of Jesus Christ the Nazarene (vv. 8-12). Then, Acts 4:13-20 records:

> When they *observed the boldness* of Peter and John and *realized that they were uneducated and untrained men, they were amazed and recognized that they had been with Jesus.* And since they saw the man who had been healed standing with them, they had nothing to say in opposition.
>
> After they ordered them to leave the Sanhedrin, they conferred among themselves, saying, "What should we do with these men? For an obvious sign has been done through them, clear to everyone living in Jerusalem, and we cannot deny it. But so that this does not spread any further among the people, let's threaten them against speaking to anyone in this name again."
>
> So they called for them and ordered them not to speak or teach at all in the name of Jesus. *Peter and John answered them, "Whether it's right in the sight of God for us to listen to you rather than to God, you decide; for we are*

unable to stop speaking about what we have seen and heard"
(emphasis added).

Notice that the members of the Sanhedrin observe in amazement Peter and John's confidence in spite of the fact that they are both uneducated and untrained men. They attribute the apostles' confidence to the fact that they have been with Jesus.

If believers know enough of the Gospel to have been saved by it, then they know enough of the Gospel to share it with others. However, evangelistic confidence is not attained merely by what believers know (such as a memorized evangelistic script); it is attained by Whom they know (Jesus Christ).

Many believers today have received more evangelism training than those in the early church did. How, then, did early believers know what to say when they evangelized? What was the secret of their evangelistic confidence? They were with Jesus (v. 13). They remembered what they had seen (v. 20). They recalled what they had heard (v. 20). Those seeking evangelistic confidence will find it whenever they spend time with Jesus. Those who spend time with Jesus cannot help but spend time telling others about Jesus. In addition, those with whom we spend time telling about Jesus can tell whether we spend time with Jesus (v. 13).

Well-known evangelist J. Harold Smith came to serve as the pastor of the First Baptist Church of Fort Smith, Arkansas, in 1953. Smith was a man who walked with God, as evidenced by the fact that he, like Peter and John, confidently told almost everyone with whom he came into contact about Jesus Christ. Not long after assuming his new pastorate, Smith heard about Ken Boen. Despite Boen's reputation of having a hardened heart to the Gospel, Smith paid him a visit at his home. He was not confident that Boen would receive Christ, but he was confident that Jesus would be with him when he went.

Dressed in his best Sunday suit and shoes, Smith gingerly stepped around and over the mud puddles to meet Boen, who was in the field tending to his horses. Boen listened to the pastor-evangelist as he shared the Gospel with him. Smith then asked him if he would be willing to receive Jesus Christ as his Lord and Savior. Boen's eyes scanned the preacher from his head to his feet, looked at the mud puddles all around him, and then peered deeply into Smith's eyes. He replied, "Preacher, if you're willing to bend down on your knees with me to pray right now, then I'm willing to receive Christ right now." With no hesitation at all, Smith confidently bent down in the mud. Though the evangelist's clean suit and shoes became a muddy mess, the steer wrestler's filthy heart was made clean as he, too, bent to his knees and received Jesus Christ as his Savior and Lord.

– Matt Queen

Guided Prayer:

- Thank God for the power that Jesus' name has to save sinners.
- Ask God to use the time you have with Him to help you boldly proclaim Jesus to someone else.
- Pray that God will illumine your eyes as you study His Word so that, like Peter and John, you will not be able to stop speaking about all you have read.

DAY 11

ACTS 6-7

Main Idea: *We are all called to proclaim the Gospel, regardless of our specific role in the church.*

When we think of the preaching crusades of Billy Graham, we understand that in order for him to stand and proclaim the Gospel, there were many others who were involved behind the scenes serving at each event. Without being present to see it all happen, we can wonder how much these servants were also involved in sharing the Gospel.

Some for sure were counselors who followed up with a further explanation of the Gospel. Others may have been more focused on practical aspects such as seating, sound systems, and parking. All of this combined to produce an evangelistic event where the Gospel was declared to many.

So let us consider: Is it okay for us to be among these supporting servants who enable gifted evangelists to share the Gospel *without actually sharing the Gospel ourselves*?

As we read of the expanding church in the book of Acts, we get to chapters 6 and 7, where there are growing pains. This new church has practical issues such as caring for the various new Christians—in particular, the widows. The twelve apostles are involved in a lot of ministry, and now they have to pay attention to practical issues as well. The obvious solution is to find others who can serve behind the scenes and take care of these practical matters. So they appoint seven men who are able to oversee all of these practical arrangements. This is not a random appointment, but rather, we read how they are chosen based on proven character.

But do these servant overseers work *only* behind the scenes to support the apostles as they share the Gospel? If we end the story here, then this certainly appears to be the model. But the story continues with a focus on one of these behind-the-scenes servants, namely Stephen. Not only does he fulfill the duty to oversee practical situations, but we read how he is clearly involved in declaring the truth of the Gospel to the point that he is arrested. Even in this difficult situation, in Acts 7, he preaches an amazing message summarizing the Old Testament and linking it all to Christ and the Gospel. He is so passionate and convicting that he ends up paying the ultimate price. In Stephen, we have someone who is supposedly in the shadow of the apostles and yet who is known for his proclamation of the Gospel.

If we were to find out more about a Billy Graham crusade, we would discover a culture of Gospel proclamation where everyone involved was encouraged to share the Gospel in whatever situation the Lord placed them. If the Lord gives you a public platform, then use it to proclaim the Gospel. If the Lord has you behind the scenes, then use every opportunity to proclaim the Gospel.

We can be tempted to think that if we are not gifted evangelists with a public platform, we simply need to support those who have this gift without being personally involved in proclaiming the Gospel. While it is biblically correct that we all have different gifts, it is not biblically correct to say that only some gifted believers are to share the Gospel. Stephen is an example and an encouragement for all of us to be involved in sharing the Gospel.

Two significant principles in his story can help us apply this truth. First, **Stephen's witness is founded on his character**—specifically, how the Lord produces Christlikeness in him. Throughout his story, we read of words and phrases like "full of the Spirit and wisdom" (6:3), "full of faith and the Holy Spirit" (6:5), and "full of grace and power" (6:8). Stephen does not witness in his own strength but rather from a growing walk with Jesus. We can try to witness in our own strength; however, the closer we walk with Jesus, the more effective our witness will be.

Second, **Stephen is not jealous of the apostles**. We find no evidence that he is unhappy with his appointment to serve or that he envies the apostles, who do not need to serve as he does. One of the big discouragements to witnessing is when we compare ourselves with others. We are all called to be faithful witnesses right where the Lord has placed us, and rather than compare, we should encourage others to be faithful where they find themselves and all praise the Lord when He brings a harvest.

From the time of the early church, it was clear that all Christians were involved in sharing the Gospel, not only in behind-the-scenes work, but also in terms of a personal witness. We live in a time where people have many challenges, and it is still relevant to serve others in any way we can. As with Stephen, this must also be accompanied by a clear verbal presentation of the Gospel, which, in the end, is the best service we can give to anyone. Let us love people with acts of service and the words of life.

– Dean Sieberhagen

Guided Prayer:

- Thank God for providing everyone with opportunities to proclaim the Gospel, whether they serve publicly or behind the scenes.
- Pray that God will help you grow in Christlikeness through a closer walk with Him, that your witness may be as effective as it can be.
- Pray that God will help you to be humble in accepting the role that He has assigned to you and using it to proclaim the Gospel.

DAY 12

ACTS 8:1-4

Main Idea: *Persecution is a catalyst for a wider spread of the Gospel.*

Something stirred in Jerusalem in the early decades of the first century. One from meager roots but a rich lineage, a carpenter's son named Jesus, died and was buried in a borrowed tomb, then rose from the dead and was seen by many witnesses. He brought eternity-altering truth, changing human reality and enacting what God decided before the foundation of the world. He was the God-Man.

Other commoners followed and converted yet others until the momentum of this message threatened governing officials, both Jewish and Roman. These commoners arose and eventually paid the ultimate price for truth. Eusebius, the third-century historian, indicated that all of the original apostles, except for John, were martyred. Stephen was the first among these heroes of the faith.

One of the original seven deacons who assisted the apostles for ministry in the Jerusalem church, Stephen was known as an effective evangelist, powerful teacher, and miracle worker, especially among the Jews in Jerusalem. Jewish leaders plotted to snare Stephen with accusations of blasphemy against their version of Mosaic traditions. The supreme court of the Jews, the Sanhedrin, gathered, and the audience rose up to condemn him, leading to Stephen's death. Though he gave a strong rebuttal, it was so intense that his opponents "yelled at the top of their voices, covered their ears, and together rushed against him" (Acts 7:57).

As our text begins today, we learn that Saul, a leading Pharisee also known as Paul, consents to the killing (8:1). The English term hardly carries the depth of meaning. The original Greek construction is a strong term that means he takes deep, satisfying pleasure in Stephen's death. One could say he savors it with sadistic glee. The Jewish factions are furthered, and Saul takes pleasure in that.

General persecution breaks out. Both the Pharisee and the Sadducee sects set out to persecute anyone associated with Christ's followers. The word *persecute* is an old term and carries the idea of a widespread hunt, chasing down, routing out any vestiges of Christ's influences and His church.

The core apostles remain to handle the circumstances of Stephen's burial. Other believers run into Judea and Samaria and are scattered. This latter term is a strong verb meaning that definitive, coercive force is used. The word picture is of a farmer intentionally spreading grain out onto his fields. Jesus said in Acts 1:8 that believers would receive power from the Holy Spirit and would be His witnesses in Jerusalem, Judea, Samaria, and the remotest part of the earth. In one sense, this is precisely what happens. Since it is due to the direct effects of deadly persecution, one wonders if Christ's words in the first chapter are as much a prophecy of forthcoming events as a statement of fact.

Devout men bury Stephen and lament over his life and witness. Leaders of the early church, who are willing to associate their lives with Christ, and consequently with Stephen, at any cost, risk all and properly dispose of his body. *Lamentation,* or deep mourning, is an old term and used only here in the New Testament. The immensity of grief is difficult to describe. In the Old Testament's uses, it means to beat one's breast with a depth of sorrow. No one can understand unless they too have had such a life crisis.

Saul continues leading the rampage, bringing havoc to the church. He systematically goes throughout Jerusalem, pillaging homes and imprisoning believers, including women and perhaps even children.

Thus, in the wake of Stephen's death, Saul emerges as an antagonist to the things of God. He's enraged yet gleeful at the plight he brings on the followers of Christ. They face deadly persecution and are forced into other areas of the Roman world. So, out of Jerusalem, believers run initially into Judea and Samaria, into the regions Christ predicted, to begin the worldwide spread of the eternity-altering truths of Jesus Christ, especially His life, death, burial, resurrection, and imminent return. Indeed, those who are scattered go about preaching the Word (8:4). What men intended for evil, God uses for good, for as the believers are scattered, so is the message of Christ.

Another of God's ironic twists in the story is that the lead persecutor, Saul, eventually refocuses his zeal to become the leading protagonist for Christ's causes after a conversion experience on the road to Damascus (Acts 9:1-22). God makes all things work together for His purposes and good. God blunts the main hammer pounding the church and turns him into a plowshare for the soils of the church throughout most of the known world.

Today, many believers face similar degrees of persecution as the early church. The underground churches in China, Christians facing the rampage of ruthless Islamic factions like the Boko Haram in West Africa, the beatings or burnings in parts of India, or those simply standing up for Christian truths in parts of the world where there are free legal options. But just as with the early church, such persecution is not quashing worldwide Christian witness; it is enhancing it. Despite men's best efforts, the Gospel continues to spread, for wherever the persecuted believers go, they continue to preach the Word. Whether in the first century or the 21st century, persecution is a catalyst for a wider spread of the Gospel, so long as believers maintain their focus on things eternal, as Stephen did (Acts 7:55-56).

Brothers and sisters, what would your church today look like if believers lived with their vision focused solely on life in the next world rather than on the here and now? Let each of us ask ourselves, "What do I need to put on the altar for God's purposes in my own life (Romans 12:1-2)?" Perhaps there would be more transformed angelic faces, like the Sanhedrin saw in Stephen's face (Acts 6:15), if we too were willing to place our lives completely in the hands of Christ.

– Keith E. Eitel

Guided Prayer:

- Thank God that He works everything for our good, which is our reconciliation to Him for His glory and praise.
- Pray for the persecuted believers around the world, that God will protect them, grant them peace, and empower their witness.
- Pray that God will assist you and believers worldwide in maintaining a clear focus on the life to come rather than the things of this world.

DAY 13

ACTS 8:5-24

Main Idea: *Our witness should not be paralyzed by the possibility of false conversions.*

The experienced soul-winner knows that finding faithful converts after the passage of time provides encouragement as great as if not greater than that of their initial profession of faith. John writes, "I have no greater joy than this: to hear that my children are walking in truth" (3 John 4). Conversely, this same soul-winner also knows how deflated and discouraged he can become when he hears that those for whom he so fervently prayed and so ably witnessed have returned to the vomit (Proverbs 26:11). This reality can cause the personal evangelist to question his methods, motivation, and message, so much so that his evangelistic fire can be doused and his fervency paralyzed.

How should we proceed when we realize that some or many of those we have led to Christ have shown a false faith? One of the greatest soul-winners in the Bible dealt with this exact issue, and he provides a tremendous example for us to follow.

As a result of Stephen's martyrdom, the Christians in Jerusalem are scattered and go about preaching the word (Acts 8:4). Among them is the deacon Philip. Luke paints Philip as a man "of good reputation, full of the Spirit and wisdom," and as a hospitable father (Acts 6:3; 21:8-9). In Acts 8, Luke records his work as an evangelist.

Philip travels into Samaria and begins proclaiming the Messiah to them and preaching "the good news about the kingdom of God and the name of Jesus Christ" (Acts 8:5, 12). *Proclaiming* refers to preaching and emphasizes public evangelistic proclamation. By placing this in the imperfect tense, Luke describes this preaching ministry as an ongoing ministry, possibly similar to the protracted meetings of modern-day evangelists. Similarly, the phrase "preaching the good news" is translated from the word *euangelizo*—"to evangelize." His ministry in Samaria undoubtedly is one of evangelistic proclamation.

Luke emphasizes that while Philip is evangelizing this Samaritan city, signs accompany his ministry, including exorcisms and healings. While these miracles produce greater interest and joy among the people, they respond because of the preached Word. They believe and are baptized (v. 12). Thus, a great awakening occurs among the population of this city.

Among those caught up in this movement of God is a famous magician named Simon. Luke records that the entire city paid attention to Simon because he had amazed them with his magic. As the crowds come to Christ through Philip's ministry, Luke records that Simon also believes, and after being baptized, he continues on with Philip (v. 13). For this Gospel warrior, Simon's "conversion" could be considered the greatest victory of his evangelistic campaign. The entire city and the surrounding area would have heard of their most famous citizen's baptism. Furthermore, this celebrity begins to accompany Philip on his preaching tour.

Surely, the awakening continues to gain momentum when two of Jesus' apostles, Peter and John, visit. These two come to see what is happening and to encourage the new believers. They spend time praying over them, so that these new converts might "receive the Holy Spirit" (v. 15). While they pray for this, they lay hands on them, and the Holy Spirit is "given" to them (vv. 17-18). The old magician recognizes a power beyond his own, and his carnal heart entices him to find the secret. So, he approaches the apostles and attempts to purchase this power, presumably for his arsenal of tricks.

Peter responds to this request with as stern of words as possible. He proclaims the wrath of God against Simon, and urges him to repent and pray to God for forgiveness. Simon, however, is not willing to do so, and instead he asks the apostles to pray that he might be spared such judgment. The convert who seemed to provide so much promise and potential thus reveals what is actually occurring in his heart.

When looking back over the narrative, we can see that Luke casts doubt on the validity of Simon's "conversion" earlier on in the passage. Simon believes only *after* he sees that the whole city has fled from his audience to join Philip's. After his baptism, Simon follows Philip, and Luke is sure to point out that he "was amazed as he observed the signs and great miracles that were being performed" (v. 13). He is not concerned with the Gospel message or the lost coming to Christ. He has apparently decided to go "undercover" in order to find the secret to Philip's power. Despite the reality of this false conversion, the Spirit-led Philip does not initially discern his "belief" as false, but affirms his decision as legitimate through baptism.

Today, people respond to a Gospel invitation for many different reasons. Many are genuine responses of faith. However, many are merely outward appearances with ulterior motives. While these false conversions seem genuine in the moment, time reveals that they are not. This does not mean that the Gospel presentation or the methods employed are at fault. A great multitude was legitimately saved by Philip's ministry. We must not throw the baby out with the bathwater simply because we discover a false conversion. Philip's evangelistic zeal suffers no harm from the revelation of this false conversion (vv. 26-40).

The same sower sows the same seed that produces the trampled and the choked as well as the productive. The difference is not found in the hand of the sower, but in the heart of the soil.

– James Pritchard

Guided Prayer:

- Thank God for the opportunities He provides to proclaim Christ and preach the good news about the Kingdom of God.

- Pray that your witness will not be paralyzed by the possibility of false conversions.
- Pray that those who hear your Gospel proclamation will respond with genuine faith and later be found faithful in following the ways of the Lord. Pray for those who, like Simon, have professed faith in Christ but revealed themselves to be false converts; ask that God will bring them to true conviction, genuine repentance, and sure salvation.

DAY 14

ACTS 8:25-40

Main Idea: *The Spirit leads us to those whose hearts He has divinely prepared.*

Do you believe in divine appointments? A divine appointment is a divinely arranged and directed, life-changing encounter between two or more people. Afterward, it is not unusual for the follower of Christ to think with amazement, "Only the Lord could have made that happen!" Divine appointments can be life-changing for everyone involved, including *you*, the Gospel witness.

In Acts 8, we find just such a divine appointment. Philip has been evangelizing among the Samaritans when the Lord sends an angel to redirect him from this exciting ministry to what will be another strategic ministry on a desert road south of Jerusalem. Because Philip is the man God has prepared for this unique evangelistic opportunity, the Lord has no need to send one of the apostles. As Philip obediently follows the Lord's somewhat curious directions, he comes upon an Ethiopian official traveling on that very same road. Though initially unknown to Philip, the Lord has amazingly prepared this official's heart to receive the good news about Jesus.

That this official's heart has been prepared by God is clearly seen in his having traveled a great distance to Jerusalem to seek God in worship. His spiritual hunger is also seen in his having obtained a costly scroll of Isaiah, which he is intently studying at the very moment Philip comes upon him (v. 30). The Spirit says to Philip, "Go and join that chariot" (v. 29), thus directing him to engage the Ethiopian in a Gospel conversation. Philip's obedience to the Lord's prompting results in the salvation of this precious African soul (v. 36). God had been faithfully working in both men's lives, possibly for years, to bring everything together for this glorious result!

Why would God direct Philip away from an exciting ministry in Samaria to a divine appointment with just one man on a desert road? An early church father, Irenaeus, refers in his writings to a church tradition stating that this official embraced the joy of his newfound salvation and became an enthusiastic Gospel witness to his own African nation. What we do know for certain is that this divine appointment, and Philip's obedience to the Spirit's promptings, once again releases the Gospel to shatter racial, cultural, and national barriers for many generations to come!

Do you believe that God arranges divine appointments today in the lives of ordinary Christians? Paul writes, "For we are his workmanship, created in Christ Jesus for good works, which God prepared ahead of time for us to do" (Ephesians 2:10). Paul teaches that God faithfully prepares *each of us* in Christ for specific "works," including divine appointments, which God has planned long before these opportunities present themselves in our lives. *This thought is a strategic game changer!* As you walk through your daily routine, the Lord's unseen hand is working both to prepare you for and to guide you into these evangelistic divine appointments. The question becomes, *Will you be sensitive when His Spirit directs you to share a clear and compassionate witness to the Gospel?*

All Christians hear the voice of the Holy Spirit, even if we do not always recognize it. To help us recognize when the Spirit is pointing out these divine appointments, many believers have embraced what we might call "evangelism guidelines." When one of these guidelines occurs, we immediately look for any evangelistic opportunity the Lord may have set before us. There are several guidelines that God has used to direct me into dozens of Gospel conversations I might otherwise easily have missed.

Many believers have embraced the **Holy Spirit Guideline**. Whenever the Holy Spirit speaks to our hearts to share Christ with someone, we initiate a Gospel conversation. However, to help me better recognize when the Holy Spirit Guideline is occurring, I have embraced three supporting guidelines.

Dr. Bill Bright introduced many of us to the **Five-Minute Guideline**. If the Lord gives us a captive audience with a person for five or more minutes (like on a flight, at a ball game, or in a waiting room), we assume the Spirit is directing us to engage that person in a Gospel conversation. Another evangelism instructor suggested the **Homestead Guideline**. If God brings a stranger to our home (like a sales person, technician, delivery person, or repairman), we attempt to initiate a Gospel conversation with him. Finally, I also have my own **Detour Guideline**. If the Lord turns my life in a completely different direction than I had planned for the day (literally for me an automobile accident, an ER visit, a hospital elevator hung between two floors, a traffic ticket, and a motorcycle tow), I look to see if God has brought someone across my *new* path with whom I should initiate a Gospel conversation. With any evangelism guideline, you quickly learn the wisdom of carrying Gospel tracts with you *at all times*.

With a heart to share Jesus and with your own evangelism guidelines, most days can become an amazing adventure! Have you embraced any evangelism guidelines that the Holy Spirit can use to alert you to those evangelistic divine appointments God has purposed specifically for you? You could be amazed at how the Lord can direct your witnessing in rather astonishing ways. Philip lived this adventure. You can too!

– Charles Stewart

Guided Prayer:

- Thank God for providing a divine appointment for you to be saved. Thank God that He continues to prepare the hearts of others so that they, too, may be saved.

- Ask the Lord to direct you into divine appointments that He has prepared for you to share the Gospel with others.
- Pray that God will assist you in developing "evangelism guidelines" so that you can be a more effective witness for Him—to His glory and praise.

DAY 15

_____ **ACTS 10:1-48** _____

Main Idea: *Our evangelism should not be hindered by preconceptions or prejudices.*

A young man, after hearing a powerful message about "winning the lost for Christ," was eager to join the church's evangelism team. Immediately, the man sought out the pastor of evangelism and said with exhilaration, "I want to be obedient to the message and win souls for Christ." After going through a series of evangelism training classes, the young man was finally going to get his opportunity to win souls for Christ. To his surprise, that week's evangelism canvassing was in the slum district of the city. Upon arrival, the young man asked, "Are we going to evangelize in this area?" The pastor replied, "Yes. Is there a problem?" The young man said, "No. I just think our time could be spent best with those who want more out of life." The pastor asked the driver to turn the van around, saying, "This was a mistake." The young man said, "So we are going to head to another location?" The pastor replied, regretfully, "Son, you are not ready to win a soul for Christ until you are willing to win *any* soul for Christ."

Frequently in churches, evangelism conferences, and seminary classrooms, believers affirm that "God created every person in His image." Undeniably, a basic understanding of this statement warrants that Christians be willing to evangelize anyone. Sadly, however, some believers find difficulty evangelizing all human beings created by God due to preconceptions or prejudices.

Acts 10 records the story of Cornelius, "a centurion of what was called the Italian Regiment ... a devout man [who] feared God along with his whole household [and] did many charitable deeds for the Jewish people and always prayed to God" (vv. 1-2). Observing his efforts, God instructs Cornelius to seek out His servant Peter (vv. 3-6). While Cornelius' servants seek for Peter, God allows Peter to fall into a trance. Peter then experiences the following vision:

> He saw heaven opened and an object that resembled a large sheet coming down, being lowered by its four corners to the earth. In it were all the four-footed animals and reptiles of the earth, and the birds of the sky. A voice said to him, "Get up, Peter; kill and eat." "No, Lord!" Peter said. "For I have never eaten anything impure and ritually unclean." Again, a second time, the voice said to him, "What God has made clean, do not call impure." This happened three times, and suddenly the object was taken up into heaven (vv. 11-16).

While Peter is still "deeply perplexed" as to what this vision means, Cornelius' servants arrive, and, led by the Spirit, Peter accepts their invitation to accompany them to Cornelius' house (vv. 17-23). There, Peter says to Cornelius and to the many people assembled there, "You know it's forbidden for a Jewish man to associate with or visit a foreigner, but God has shown me that I must not call any person impure or unclean. That's why I came without any objection when I was sent for" (vv. 28-29a).

Notice Peter's prejudice against Cornelius, who is a Gentile. Peter previously saw Gentiles as unholy. And yet he willingly comes to Cornelius' house without objection. What does Peter teach us through this encounter? He informs us that prejudices and preconceptions against others should not prevent us from sharing the Gospel. After all, our sin did not stop God from hearing our cry, so why should prejudices or preconceptions prevent us from hearing others'? Peter comes to realize that salvation is available to all: "Now I truly understand that God doesn't show favoritism, but in every nation the person who fears him and does what is right is acceptable to him" (vv. 34-35).

What prejudices and preconceptions do you hold? Do you allow stereotypes to hinder your evangelism to certain people? Or, more importantly, do you let your prejudices keep you from evangelism altogether? As those who have been accepted by God, may we also receive every sinner as worthy of hearing the Gospel of Jesus Christ, which is available to all people from every nation who fear the Lord.

– Carl J. Bradford

Guided Prayer:

- Thank God for accepting you as one of His own, despite your being "unholy."
- Repent of any prejudices or preconceptions that you have against others, and especially of those instances in which such prejudices and preconceptions hindered your evangelistic witness.
- Pray that God will soften your heart to people from every nation, tribe, people, and tongue so that nothing will hinder your evangelism.

DAY 16

Main Idea: *The Holy Spirit assists us with the means to face spiritual opposition.*

The following warning is now popular in the business world: "Culture eats strategy for breakfast." A strategy can indeed be important, but culture can easily overpower strategy. Similarly, Satan can easily overpower well-intentioned but carnal Christians who try to fight him in a fleshly way. In contrast, Christians can experience successful spiritual warfare when the Spirit works through them.

To become Christians, people must surrender their lives to Christ in repentance and faith. After that initial commitment, Christians have eternal life with Christ and cannot lose it. After conversion, however, Christians must struggle against the impulses of their old sinful nature. The issue is not how much of the Spirit the believer has; rather, the issue is how much of the believer the Spirit has. On a daily basis, Christians should properly prepare for spiritual warfare. They must submit all situations to God, confess known sins, and ask for deliverance from Satan's attacks. This daily preparation is especially important for effective witnessing, an activity that Satan vehemently opposes.

Consider the opposition encountered by Paul and Barnabas and the spiritual victory they see in Acts 13:4-12. After proclaiming the Word of God in the Jewish synagogues (v. 5), they are summoned by the proconsul, Sergius Paulus, "an intelligent man" (v. 7). This man explicitly desires to hear the Word of God—what a great opportunity for evangelism! And yet, Paul and Barnabas still experience difficulty.

This difficulty comes in the form of Elymas, also known as Bar-Jesus, a magician. While Paul and Barnabas attempt to evangelize the proconsul, Elymas opposes them and tries "to turn the proconsul away from the faith" (v. 8). The Scripture leaves no doubt that this opposition is satanic in nature—Paul refers to Elymas as a "son of the devil" and an "enemy of all that is right" (v. 10). Thus, we see in this passage a clear example of spiritual warfare.

And how do Paul and Barnabas overcome this challenge to their witness? Do they use worldly means to overpower Elymas—fine-sounding arguments, flattering words, or physical force? No. For they realize that this struggle "is not against flesh and blood, but against the rulers, against the authorities, against the cosmic powers of this darkness, against evil, spiritual forces in the heavens" (Ephesians 6:12). Therefore, they do not use the weapons of this world, but rather the power of God.

Filled with the Holy Spirit, Paul fixes his gaze on Elymas and says to him, "You are full of all kinds of deceit and trickery, … won't you ever stop perverting the straight paths of the Lord? Now, look, the Lord's hand is against you. You are going to be blind, and will not see the sun for a time" (Acts 13:9-11a). Immediately, "a mist and darkness" fall upon Elymas, and he seeks someone to "lead him by the hand" (v. 11b). The proconsul, seeing this demonstration of spiritual power and hearing the Word of God, believes the witness.

While the Holy Spirit will likely not strike our opponents blind as He did Elymas, He nevertheless continues to assist our witness when we face spiritual opposition in our evangelism today. Indeed, He provides us spiritual armor, that we may "stand against the schemes of the devil" (Ephesians 6:11). This armor consists of truth, righteousness, readiness, faith, salvation, prayer, and the sword of the Spirit itself, the Word of God (vv. 14-18). Armed with such weapons for spiritual warfare, we can stand firm (vv. 11, 13, 14), and our witness may proceed with boldness as we proclaim the mystery of the Gospel (vv. 19-20).

Paul provides a great example of this in his encounter with Elymas. Filled with the Spirit, he achieves victory in the spiritual battle, and the proconsul is won to Christ. May we seek to be filled with the Spirit as well, that we may see similar results in our evangelism.

And how can we be so filled? By daily preparing for spiritual warfare. By committing ourselves to prayer—submitting all situations to God, confessing known sins, and asking for deliverance from Satan's attacks. Jesus mentions these elements in the model prayer—"Your will be done," "forgive us our debts," and "deliver us from the evil one" (Matthew 6:9-13). And finally, by studying God's Word. Effective Bible study helps Christians to discern evil and explain God's plan of salvation. The sword of the Spirit is our most powerful weapon in spiritual warfare.

So, brothers and sisters, let us utilize these tools from the Lord, that we may be filled with the Spirit; that He may have all of who we are. Then we will be able to evangelize with all boldness, knowing that the Holy Spirit will be at work in us and through us every step of the way, giving us victory in spiritual battles and winning souls to Christ. Lord, may it be so!

– Mike Morris and Alex Sibley

Guided Prayer:

- Thank the Lord for giving you His Holy Spirit, who assists you with the means to face spiritual opposition.
- Commit yourself to daily prayer and Bible study, that you may be filled with the Spirit and that He may have all of who you are.
- Ask the Lord for wisdom and boldness as you use the armor of God and the sword of the Spirit to stand firm in spiritual warfare during your evangelism.

DAY 17

ACTS 13:13-52

Main Idea: *Even when rejected, the Gospel can lead to joy.*

Rejection comes in many forms. Sometimes, it's the rustle of a curtain in a window as someone sneaks a peek to see who rang the doorbell. But the door never opens. Other times, it's an excuse—"Oh, we're just heading out," or, "We're just coming in," or, "No English." Each of those things could be true, and we don't ever try to figure out when they are or are not, but deep down, we also know that, sometimes, it's just rejection. On rare occasions, it might even be something more hurtful—harsh words when we ask when might be a good time to return and the answer is, "How about never." But even though all of this rejection can hurt, sometimes the worst hurt we feel is when we clearly present the Gospel, they listen, our fellow evangelists pray, and then … they just say "no."

But does rejection only bring with it hurt? Is it only discouraging when we knock and present and pray and hope and no one believes? Sometimes, it feels that way, but when we find ourselves on those days, when it seems no one will believe, when we give our best to the Lord in the work of evangelism and there just aren't any takers, we can take heart in this thought: *Even when rejected, the Gospel can lead to joy.* It says it right there in Acts 13:13-52.

Paul and Barnabas find themselves in a synagogue in Pisidian Antioch on their first missionary journey. They are even invited by the leaders to share a word of exhortation. Being the scholar that he is and knowing his audience will follow well his line of presentation, Paul lays out for the Israelites the entire history of their people. He gives them everything from Egypt to the desert wanderings to the conquering of the Promised Land to the judges to the kings to John the Baptist and Jesus. He even presents the death, burial, and resurrection of Christ and the fulfillment of prophecy in the Gospel. This all appears to be going great at the end of that first day when Paul is invited back the next Sabbath to speak again. But then the rejection begins.

When Paul returns, the whole city has gathered to hear more about Jesus, but the Jews become jealous, even going so far as to accuse Paul of blasphemy. This kind of rejection can certainly lead to despair and hurt and doubt about one's abilities, but that isn't how Paul and Barnabas take it. They understand that this rejection is exactly the thing that will send them out to the ends of the earth to reach the Gentiles with the Gospel. And that will lead to much joy!

Notice in verse 48 the joy that this rejection brings: "When the Gentiles heard this, they rejoiced and honored the word of the Lord, and all who had been appointed to eternal life believed." Of course, the Gentiles aren't rejoicing in the rejection of the Gospel by the Jews, but rather in the joy that salvation brings to them: knowing that not only can they be saved, but their families can be saved; and not only can their families be saved, but all of the peoples of the whole earth—anyone who believes!

The text goes on to say that the "word of the Lord spread through the whole region" (v. 49). And even though more persecution comes from the Jews and more rejection by the leading men and women of the city, Paul and Barnabas shake the dust off their feet and travel on with the Gospel to the next region. "And the disciples were filled with joy and the Holy Spirit" (v. 52).

So, brothers and sisters, the next time you see that rustle in the window or hear a kind rejection or maybe even a harsh one, just remember Paul and Barnabas and their time in Pisidian Antioch. Remember that when one person rejects the Gospel, it just means you're going to get to share the Gospel with someone else and someone else and someone else after that.

What about that family ten houses down who's waiting for you to share the Gospel with them? What if you didn't get rejected nine times before that? All those rejections have brought you here to their home. You're here at just the right time and just the right place to share with them. When they receive the Word with faith, it will mean their joy—and yours, too.

– Mark Leeds

Guided Prayer:

- Thank the Lord for always providing further opportunities to share the Gospel, even in the wake of rejection.
- Pray that when you are evangelizing, the Holy Spirit will call to your mind this story of Paul and Barnabas, who continued spreading the Gospel even after facing persecution, and witnessed the joyous salvation of the lost.
- Pray that those who hear your message will not harden their hearts, but rather receive it with joy and respond with repentance and faith.

DAY 18

─────── **ACTS 14:1-7** ───────

Main Idea: *The Lord bears witness to our bold proclamation.*

The preacher said every believer should wake up each day and pray this prayer: "Lord, give me an opportunity today to share the Gospel with someone. Lord, help me recognize the opportunity to share the Gospel when you provide it. Finally, Lord, give me the boldness to act on the opportunity to share the Gospel."

From the first moment I heard this prayer, I have not forgotten it. This prayer speaks to the essence of Jesus' purpose for each one of us. This prayer reminds us of our commission as Christians. This prayer claims us as ambassadors and witnesses for Christ who are called to speak the Gospel.

The opportunity to speak the Gospel is one of the greatest privileges every Christian has been given. While an opportunity, it is also a command that our love for Christ and for the lost compels us to obey. Yet, to obey this command is to willingly step to the front lines of a cosmic battle raging between heaven and hell. What provision exists for such a conflict? What strength and resources are available to secure victory? Why should you soldier on and fight this good fight? Read the following account of Paul and Barnabas from the book of Acts to find out:

> In Iconium they entered the Jewish synagogue, as usual, and spoke in such a way that a great number of both Jews and Greeks believed. But the unbelieving Jews stirred up the Gentiles and poisoned their minds against the

brothers. So they stayed there a long time and spoke boldly for the Lord, who testified to the message of his grace by enabling them to do signs and wonders.

But the people of the city were divided, some siding with the Jews and others with the apostles. When an attempt was made by both the Gentiles and Jews, with their rulers, to mistreat and stone them, they found out about it and fled to the Lycaonian towns of Lystra and Derbe and to the surrounding countryside. There they continued preaching the gospel (Acts 14:1-7).

Paul and Barnabas might not have prayed the exact prayer mentioned above, but they obviously committed their days to speaking the Gospel. Without a doubt, they prayed for the opportunity to speak the Gospel on this particular day, to see their opportunity, and to have the boldness to act on their opportunity. Keep in mind, they had just been driven out of Pisidian Antioch for speaking the Gospel! Undeterred, on to the next city they went with full resolve to share the Good News of Jesus Christ.

When Paul and Barnabas speak the Gospel in Iconium, they see incredible results—a multitude of both Jews and Greeks believe! In other words, a great number of people respond to their message by placing their faith in Jesus Christ. Truth goes forth and pierces the darkness. Lost souls held in bondage to sin walk free by faith! Remember, faith comes by hearing (Romans 10:17). This is why they speak the Gospel, and why we must as well.

Are you in the habit of speaking the Gospel? If so, what happens in verse 2 does not come as a shock. Despite the great multitude who do believe, a great number remains who do not. Even worse, a group of Jewish leaders actively seek to destroy Paul and Barnabas' reputation among the unbelievers. This opposition does not surprise Paul and Barnabas. They know their message confronts and exposes the darkness of sin and unbelief. They know the enemy will fight back. What about you? Are you surprised when opposition arises because of your obedience to God's commands? Have you forgotten that you are in a battle?

Once Paul and Barnabas realize the fierceness of the opposition in Iconium, they do not leave. In fact, the escalating retaliation serves to strengthen their resolve and confirm their purpose. They dig in. Do you dig in? When opposition to your faith arises and the liabilities of speaking your faith increase, do you stay in the fight or flee?

Acts 14:3 says Paul and Barnabas stay in the battle to speak the Gospel. They stay in the battle until they are likely to lose their lives. Only then, out of prudence, do they leave to continue the battle elsewhere. What holds them in the battle? Who comes to their aid? Who testifies to their message with miraculous signs and wonders? The Lord Himself does! Paul and Barnabas obey their commission to speak boldly for the Lord, and the Lord keeps His promise to affirm the truth of their message. Truly, *the Lord bears witness to our bold proclamation!*

Every time the word of grace—the Gospel; the good news of the riches of salvation through Christ—is spoken, the Lord, by the power of the Holy Spirit, bears witness to it. In this case, He does so by granting visible signs and wonders. Physical and visible miracles, however, are not the only way the Lord bears witness to His word. The primary way the Holy Spirit bears witness to His word is by convicting of sin, opening spiritually blind eyes, imparting faith, and drawing unbelievers to Himself.

We speak the word to the ears, while God simultaneously speaks to the heart. In this way, witnessing to the truth with our lips unleashes the work and witness of the Holy Spirit. Yes, when we speak the Gospel, we engage in the battle. Yet, the witness of the Holy Spirit wins the battle. Be bold today! Engage in the battle today! Take confidence today that the Lord will bear witness to your witness.

– C. Kyle Walker

Guided Prayer:

- Thank God that He bears witness to our bold proclamation, encouraging and empowering us for the task of evangelism.

- Ask that God would give you the opportunity today to share the Gospel, that you would see the opportunity, and that you would act on the opportunity.
- Ask God to give you resolve in the face of opposition to continue sharing the Good News of Jesus Christ.

DAY 19

ACTS 14:8-20

Main Idea: *Our evangelism must be marked by humility even in the midst of flattery.*

"That was a good sermon!"

"I've never heard someone teach as well as you!"

"Your evangelism is so fruitful—how do you do it?"

Perhaps you have heard statements like these in the past. Indeed, those who operate in the power of the Holy Spirit are likely to hear such compliments, for people often fail to realize the true source of great preaching, teaching, and evangelism. Spirit-led servants know that they are just that—Spirit-led—but recipients and observers of their ministry sometimes fail to recognize such a thing and instead pay compliments to the ministers themselves, not understanding that these ministers are merely mouthpieces of God, conduits through which the Holy Spirit speaks and moves.

So what should we do when we receive such compliments? The answer may seem obvious, but that does not lessen the temptation posed in this scenario. When someone pays us a compliment, the temptation is to take that compliment for ourselves, allowing our ego to be inflated and our pride to grow. And if we give in to that temptation even once, it will become easier to give in a second time, and then a third, and before long, we will be taking all the credit for what God is doing through us. In short, we will be stealing the glory and honor that are due to Him alone.

Brothers and sisters, may it be clearly understood that pride in the ministry is a dangerous sin against the Lord that can bear horrible ramifications for ourselves, our families, our churches, and our ministries. We must therefore guard ourselves against such sin. But how do we do such a thing? What tools or precedents has God provided in the Scripture for our instruction in this matter?

Consider the story of Paul and Barnabas in Lystra in Acts 14. Verses 8-10 provide the setup. After arriving in Lystra, Paul finds a man lame since birth, who listens to Paul's message. Seeing that he has "faith to be healed," Paul fixes his gaze upon him and says with a loud voice, "Stand up on your feet!" (vv. 9-10a). Instantaneously, this man, who has never walked, not only stands, but leaps to his feet and begins to walk (v. 10b). A miracle truly takes place.

In verse 11, a complication arises. When the crowds see what Paul has done, they raise their voice and shout, "The gods have come down to us in human form!" Verse 12 says that they begin to call Barnabas, Zeus, and Paul, Hermes. The priest of Zeus even brings bulls and wreaths to the gates, "intend[ing], with the crowds, to offer sacrifice" (v. 13).

What is happening in Lystra this day? After seeing the miracle, the people fail to recognize that Paul is merely an instrument used by the Lord to heal the man lame since birth, and they mistakenly conclude that Paul is the one who has healed him. In other words, the people mistake the vessel of the Holy Spirit's power for the source of the power. They fail to understand that Paul does not minister in his own power, but rather by the power of God.

Being mistaken for gods certainly has potential to feed the pride of Paul and Barnabas, and the people's awe, praise, and accolades have potential to tickle their ears and warm their hearts. The apostles may well be tempted to keep this praise for themselves. But they do not give in. They do not allow themselves to be flattered. They do not allow the sin of pride to swell up within them. Instead, they set a precedent for how to overcome such temptation: **they humble themselves and direct all attention and praise to the Lord**.

In response to the people's blasphemous praise, Paul and Barnabas tear their robes—a symbolic gesture of their grief over the people's idolatry. They then explain to the crowd that they are but men, not gods, of the same nature as the Lystrans themselves. Indeed, the Scripture itself specifies earlier in this chapter of Acts that Paul and Barnabas do not perform miracles of their own power, but *the Lord* enables them to do signs and wonders (v. 3). The apostles are merely conduits through which the Spirit works; they operate not in their own power, but His power flows through them.

Next, the apostles explicitly exhort the people to turn from their idolatrous ways to the living God, "who made the heaven, the earth, the sea, and everything in them" (v. 15). They then emphasize God's goodness displayed to the Lystrans, who have experienced "rain from heaven and fruitful seasons," and have been filled with food and joy (v. 17). Thus, the apostles not only humble themselves, but also direct the people's attention to where it rightly belongs—to the Lord God Almighty, who displays His power and goodness to all inhabitants of the earth.

When the temptation of pride arises, Paul and Barnabas do not give it time to fester within them. Instead, they set a precedent that all modern-day evangelists would do well to follow: they immediately humble themselves and direct all praise to God. Brothers and sisters, may we do likewise. When our sermons or Sunday School lessons or evangelistic practices are complimented, may we immediately acknowledge that every positive result of our ministry is ultimately a result of God's hand of blessing upon us. Without Him, we are nothing. He is the vine; we are merely branches. And only through abiding in Him can we bear fruit (John 15:5). We thus deserve no accolades—all praise and glory and honor belong to Him and Him alone.

A final word of caution is implicitly offered at the conclusion of this story. Following their initial interaction with the apostles, the Lystrans—those who insisted on offering sacrifices to Paul and Barnabas, thinking them to be gods—are incited by Jews from Antioch and Iconium and stone Paul nearly to death and drag him out of the city (v. 19). The very people who praise Paul and Barnabas in the morning turn on them in the evening. The praises of men prove fleeting, and their affections, fickle. Clearly, we cannot rely on human accolades, for the well of man's affections runs dry quickly and, often, without warning. So may we not aim to please men and earn their praises, but rather minister in the power of God to the praise of God, humbly acknowledging that we are His mouthpieces and nothing more.

– Alex Sibley

Guided Prayer:

- Thank God for appointing you as a vessel and a mouthpiece for Him.
- Repent of those times when you stole the glory and honor due only to God.
- Pray that when you face the temptation of pride in the midst of flattery, you will immediately humble yourself and direct all attention and praise to the Lord.

DAY 20

ACTS 16:11-15

Main Idea: *God is the most important agent in our evangelism.*

Oftentimes in our evangelism, we focus heavily on conversation-starters, transitions, different ways of presenting the Gospel, and effective invitations. A consideration of such aspects of our evangelism is certainly not uncalled for, and we would do well to ponder the most effective means of accomplishing each of these steps in our intentional interactions with unbelievers. However, by getting so caught up in these finer details of evangelistic conversations, we often betray a misunderstanding of the most important component of all.

Let me clarify my meaning in the form of a question: Who is the most important agent in our evangelism? When we put so much emphasis on *our* role in the process—that is, how *we* will conduct the conversation—we are acting as though the results of our evangelism depend on us. While we may not affirm such a notion explicitly, we do so functionally when we put too much stress upon the details of conducting a conversation.

Again, I submit that such details are not unimportant, and effort should be devoted to thinking through these steps. But, is that the most important thing? Again I ask: Who is the most important agent in our evangelism?

Consider the story of Lydia's conversion in Acts 16. Here is the story in its entirety as recounted in the text of Scripture:

> On the Sabbath day we went outside the city gate by the river, where we expected to find a place of prayer. We sat down and spoke to the women gathered there. A God-fearing woman named Lydia, a dealer in purple cloth from the city of Thyatira, was listening. The Lord opened her heart to respond to what Paul was saying. After she and her household were baptized, she urged us, "If you consider me a believer in the Lord, come and stay at my house." And she persuaded us (vv. 13-15).

Notice what is *not* included in this account. No mention is made of Paul's use of an effective conversation-starter; a clever transition into spiritual things; a powerful presentation of the story of Jesus' life, death, and resurrection; or a compelling invitation to respond to the Gospel message. Does Paul's evangelistic encounter with Lydia include such elements? Likely, yes. But the emphasis of the text is not on Paul's role in Lydia's conversion. Rather, the most active agent in this story is said to be God Himself: "*the Lord* opened her heart to respond" (v. 14b, emphasis added).

The text, crucially, does clarify that Paul speaks a message to Lydia (v. 13b). He does have a role to play in the process. But his is not the most important role. Indeed, we are not the most important agents in our evangelism. The most important agent is God. He is the one who opened Lydia's heart, and He is the one who opens the hearts of all nonbelievers who respond to the Gospel message. Therefore, while we should take efforts to be as effective as possible in our evangelistic interactions, we must not act as though the results depend on us. They do not. They depend on God.

Isn't this a comforting thought? Doesn't that lighten the load of the evangelistic task? God takes responsibility for the results of our evangelism. Yes, we have a role to play, but God is the most important agent. When we share the Gospel with unbelievers, the Holy Spirit is at work behind the scenes, touching their hearts and calling them to respond in repentance and faith for the forgiveness of sins and for salvation unto eternal life. That is the Spirit's role. That is the most important component of evangelism.

Consider what this truth tells us about God. Isn't He awesome?! He works to grow His Kingdom, and He has chosen to use us as the means of doing that. What a privilege! He calls us to go, but He promises to go with us. And not only that, but He will take responsibility for the results, because He will be at work behind the scenes to accomplish His purposes. Suddenly the evangelistic task doesn't seem so daunting, does it?

So yes, think about how to begin your conversations with nonbelievers. Plan how you're going to transition to the Gospel. Figure out the most effective way to share the key components of the Gospel. And articulate ahead of time how you are going to invite a response. But do this in the knowledge that these are not the most important things, for you are not the most important agent in your evangelism.

In fact, more than all of these things, perhaps you should pray that the Lord will open the hearts of these nonbelievers to whom you are planning to speak. Maybe that should be your primary focus. Pray that He will be active and that He will accomplish all that He intends. Acknowledge the Lord's role, and invite the Spirit to do His work through you.

So as you think about your evangelism, remember Lydia. Paul evangelizes to her, but he does not open her heart to respond; his is not the most important role. The most active agent in that evangelism story is also the most active agent in yours: the Lord our God.

– Alex Sibley

Guided Prayer:

- Thank God for being active in your evangelism and for taking ultimate responsibility for the results.

- Repent of any times that you elevated your role in the evangelistic process over His.
- Pray that God will open the hearts of those who hear your message, understanding that this is the most important component of evangelism.

DAY 21

ACTS 16:25-34

Main Idea: *In addition to our proclamation, we should consider our life-witness to unbelievers, particularly in view of difficult and trying situations.*

Difficult and trying situations are never an acceptable excuse to disobey God. Unfortunately, we sometimes believe that if life is difficult, then we can be anxious, hateful, and self-centered; but this is far from the truth. In fact, Jesus provides the perfect example of obeying God through difficult and trying situations. When He hung on the cross, He continued to trust in God. He consistently loved others. He was concerned for the salvation of the lost (Luke 23:34, 39-43).

In Acts 16:25-34, Paul and Silas provide a brilliant example of imitating Christ. After dismissing a spirit of divination from a slave-girl, enduring the uproar of the locals' love for money, and being stripped of their robes and beaten with rods, they find themselves locked in the inner prison of a Philippian jail. Their feet are fastened in the stocks, and fellow prisoners surround them. But even at the end of an exhausting day, Paul and Silas do not second-guess their decisions, talk carelessly about the angry crowd, or complain about their wounds. Instead, they have their minds on Christ.

In the midst of this trial, Paul and Silas love God. The Scripture states, "About midnight Paul and Silas were praying and singing hymns to God, and the prisoners were listening to them" (v. 25). Whether they pray for freedom, souls to be won, healing, or food, we do not know. However, we do know that God sends an earthquake. This earthquake shakes the foundations of the prison. It shakes the prison doors open.

It shakes the chains off of every prisoner. But it does not shake the faith of our brothers.

In the midst of this trial, Paul and Silas love others. When the jailer sees that the doors are open, he supposes that the prisoners have escaped, and so he decides to kill himself. But then Paul cries out, "Don't harm yourself, because we're all here!" (v. 28). Paul looks with compassion upon the jailer, who had thrown them into the inner prison and chained them up. After confirming Paul's declaration, the jailer brings Paul and Silas out of the prison and asks them the sweetest question: "What must I do to be saved?" (v. 30).

The Bible does not specifically state why the jailer asks such a question. Neither Paul and Silas' evangelism in the city, nor their prayers and songs to God, nor their lifestyle, nor the slave-girl's proclamation, nor the earthquake, nor the jailer's attempt to take his own life receive direct credit for the jailer's question. The Bible also does not state that believers should wait to hear this question before they share the Gospel. The Bible just states that he asks about salvation. The jailer, who is imprisoned by sin, asks those imprisoned by him for freedom.

In the midst of this trial, Paul and Silas are concerned about the salvation of the lost. They respond as any believer should to this question. They give the jailer a command to believe in the Lord Jesus. A promise of salvation accompanies this command. Specifically, they state, "Believe in the Lord Jesus, and you will be saved—you and your household" (v. 31). Following this command and promise, they speak the word of the Lord to the jailer and to his household (v. 32).

The jailer takes Paul and Silas and washes their wounds. He and all his household, having believed in the Lord Jesus, are baptized. Then, he brings his brothers-in-Christ into his home to eat and rejoices greatly about his and his family's salvation in Jesus Christ.

Paul and Silas demonstrate the strength of their faith while enduring hardship. Not only do they love God, but they love others and are concerned for the salvation of the lost. In this trial, God blesses them with freedom, healing, food, and the salvation of the jailer and his whole household.

Our love for God and for others, including our desire to save the lost, should not wither during adversity, but we should find it flourishing. On the edge of our lips, we should hold firmly the proclamation, "Believe in the Lord Jesus, and you will be saved!" Do not miss the opportunity to worship God, love others, and win souls during difficult and trying situations. Let anxiety, hatefulness, and self-centeredness not even be named among you. May our worship never cease, our compassion never expire, and our verbal witness never become reticent.

– Jonathan Baldwin

Guided Prayer:

- Thank God that He is able to use difficult and trying situations to save the lost.
- Repent of any anxiety, hatefulness, or self-centeredness that you have experienced in the midst of trials. Ask God to open your eyes to the work that He may have for you to do in such times.
- Pray that the Holy Spirit will help you to remain a consistent and faithful witness even in difficult situations, and that this faithfulness will lead to Gospel proclamation and salvation for the lost.

DAY 22

ACTS 17:10-12

Main Idea: *Belief in Jesus occurs when an eager soul meets a determined Christian with an open Bible and an urgent mission.*

Consider the term "picture-perfect." The expression carries the idea of a faultless image lacking defects or flaws; it refers to that which is ideal. Photographers know that a "picture-perfect" snapshot requires utmost attention to detail:

> *Set the camera's focus.*
> *Use leading lines.*
> *Look for symmetry.*
> *Capture small details.*
> *Find different perspectives.*
> *Embrace empty space.*
> *Use natural light.*
> *Create abstracts.*
> *Keep an eye out for repetitive patterns.*

These are all essential techniques used by professional photographers. However, before the ideal picture comes to life, the photographer must decide on the picture's format: landscape or portrait. An image displayed in landscape mode is wider than it is tall. An image displayed in portrait mode is taller than it is wide. One is a horizontal shot; the other is a vertical shot.

Did you know that the Bible is God's "picture-perfect" revelation to mankind? We know the Bible captures small details. There are even leading lines and repetitive patterns in Scripture. But the camera's focus is of primary importance. Look closely. You will see that the camera lens of Scripture sets its focus on God's plan of redemption. Jesus is the focus of Scripture. He is the locus of redemption. The Bible captures the redemptive work of Jesus in both wide-angle and vertical shots. In the Old Testament, Jesus is anticipated. In the New Testament, He is explained. The anticipation and explanation of Jesus are displayed in landscape and portrait mode throughout Scripture.

Consider Acts 17:10-12. Here, Luke provides a snapshot for the requirements of salvation. He frames the portrait of God's salvation around four key verbs. That is, the main-line verbs of Acts 17:10-12 provide the framework for the Bereans' "picture-perfect" salvation. Notice the key verbs italicized in the passage below:

> As soon as it was night, the brothers and sisters *sent* Paul and Silas away to Berea. Upon arrival, they *went* into the synagogue of the Jews. The people here were of more noble character than those in Thessalonica, since they *received* the word with eagerness and examined the Scriptures daily to see if these things were so. Consequently, many of them *believed*, including a number of the prominent Greek women as well as men (emphasis added).

The framework of this passage has four sides. There is an urgent mission (*sent*). There are determined Christians (*went*). There is an open Bible (*received the word*). There are eager souls (*believed*). In other words, the text communicates that belief in Jesus occurs when an eager soul meets a determined Christian with an open Bible and an urgent mission. And this framework recorded in Acts 17:10-12 is the same framework needed today. Consider the four sides to God's "picture-perfect" portrait of salvation:

Side #1: There is an urgent mission (v. 10a). In Acts 17, Paul is in three primary cities—Thessalonica, Berea, and Athens. While this particular passage seems to focus on the Bereans' response to the ministry of the Word Paul brings to them, the beginning of the paragraph contains a critical thought. It is not inconsequential. The text says, "As soon as it was night, the brothers and sisters sent Paul and Silas away to Berea." Two words are of utmost importance here. First, the Greek word *eutheos* (translated "as soon as," or "immediately") carries the idea "without delay or hesitation." Second, the primary Greek verb of the sentence, *ekpempo* (translated "sent"), means "to send away toward a designated goal or purpose." In other words, the text communicates that we, as Christians, have an urgent mission. We are sent away without delay or hesitation toward a designated goal. Here is the application, brothers and sisters: When the urgency of our mission is lost, complacency in our ministry will be found.

Side #2: There is a need for determined Christians (v. 10b). Notice the determination of Paul and Silas upon their arrival in Berea. The text says that "upon arrival, they went into the synagogue of the Jews." Little to no time elapses before Paul and Silas begin their work in Berea. They go to the synagogue marked by a resolved and determined spirit. The same dedication displayed by Paul and Silas is the same determination for which God looks today in you and me. The mission has not changed. The message has not changed. But, is it possible that our spirit of determination has? Brothers and sisters, share the Gospel in a spirit of determination, as if the results were all up to you; and then rest knowing that the results are all up to God.

Side #3: There is a need for an open Bible (v. 11). Consider the phrase, "they received the word with eagerness and examined the Scriptures daily to see if these things were so." Paul and Silas preach with an open Bible. They preach the text. They give the Bereans the Scriptures. And we must do the same. The Bible not only leads to salvation; it grows believers in salvation. Let us not forget that the message is more important than the messenger. Opening the Bible is more important than impressing in communication. The teacher of

God's Word can do many things, but there is one thing he must do: stay in the text. The height of arrogance is for the preacher to think he has something more to say than what God has already said in His Word. Do not deviate from the text. Scripture is not a launchpad to a better message. It is the message.

Side #4: There are eager souls ready to believe (v. 12). Look at the way the passage ends. It says, "many of them believed." Brothers and sisters, preach the Gospel to hungry souls. Only the Gospel will satisfy parched souls. We should hold the Word of God close to our hearts, but not too close that we fail to give it away. The same eagerness of the Bereans to receive the Gospel is the same eagerness people have to believe the Gospel today. We fail people when we fail to preach the Gospel. So, preach Jesus at all times. When He is in your heart, He comes out of your mouth. There is never a bad time to preach the Gospel.

So, brothers and sisters, let us remember. We have a "picture-perfect" Bible. We have a "picture-perfect" Savior. We have a "picture-perfect" redemption. Therefore, frame the picture on all sides. We have an urgent mission. We need determined Christians. We need open Bibles. There are eager souls ready to believe.

- Daniel Dickard

Guided Prayer:

- Thank God for giving us His inspired Word, which satisfies hungry souls.
- Pray that you will maintain the urgency of the mission and remain determined to preach the Word at every opportunity.
- Pray that as you preach from an open Bible, eager souls will listen and believe.

────────── **ACTS 17:16-34** ──────────

Main Idea: *Preaching the Gospel is as simple as telling others about Jesus and His resurrection from the dead.*

What extent of cultural expertise should personal evangelists possess before they evangelize? How up-to-date should they be on current trends and pop culture to communicate the Gospel to residents living in the world, whose lives are ever being conformed to the world? Must believers spend an eternity learning about this world in order that they might teach unbelievers how they can spend eternity in the world to come? Sincere, inquiring believers want to know.

A growing number of Bible scholars and writers have attempted to answer these questions by appealing to Paul's philosophical discourse on the Areopagus, or Mars Hill, in Acts 17:22-34. In the midst of Greek Epicurean and Stoic philosophers, Paul recounts that his tour of Athens' numerous temples and altars has left him with the impression that they are very religious (vv. 22-23). On one such altar he found a dedicatory inscription "To an Unknown God," and he proceeds to inform them with specifics about a deity they worship but do not know (v. 23). In addition to referring to this altar, Paul also quotes two poems, *Cretica* (v. 28a) and *Phaenomena* 5 (v. 28b), composed by the pagan poets Epimenides and Aratus, respectively.

So how does Paul preach the Christian Gospel to curious, cultural, Athenian philosophers, and what is their response? He identifies an unknown, divine being whom they worship but do not know, using it as a transition to proclaim to them a God they do not know—the Christian God who created everything in the world, determined the patterns for all the peoples of the world, and sent His righteous Son to die and be raised from the dead in order that everyone, everywhere might repent (vv. 24-31). Upon hearing about the resurrection of the dead, every hearer responds in one of three ways—many ridicule Paul; others are intrigued and desire a future conversation with him about Jesus and the resurrection; and some repent, believe, and join him as he departs (vv. 32-34).

Not a few Bible scholars and writers contend that Paul's appeal to Greek theology, art, and literature in his Areopagus speech serves as an impetus for contemporary Christians to become familiar with cultural mores in order to build a *comparative* evangelistic bridge from culture to Christ. In other words, these scholars argue that believers should attempt to evangelize secular people by comparing similarities of culture with Christ.

Certainly, knowledge about pop culture helps personal evangelists as they seek to contextualize the Gospel to their hearers. However, keep in mind that the philosophers do not invite Paul to preach Jesus and the resurrection atop the Areopagus because of the similarities he draws between their culture and his Christ. He is invited as a result of the curiosity created by his *contrastive* evangelistic presentation to the Epicurean and Stoic philosophers in the marketplace (vv. 16-21).

Paul's familiarity with Athenian theology and its worshipful architecture is not the result of an eager, educational enculturation. Instead, the city's numerous idols and altars agitate him inwardly (v. 16). In addition, the Epicureans and Stoics first hear the Gospel down in the market, not up on Mars Hill (vv. 17-20). In fact, his articulation of the Gospel prompts the philosophers to ask, "What is this ignorant show-off [lit., *seed picker*] trying to say? ... May we learn about this new teaching you are presenting?" (vv. 18-19). Their questions indicate that Paul's evangelistic contextualization of the Gospel is not *comparative* in nature, but rather *contrastive*.

Instead of relating the Athenians' religious and cultural beliefs to the Gospel, Paul contrasts the Gospel with their misunderstanding of the divine. His Gospel proclamation centers emphatically on Jesus and His resurrection. However, several of the philosophers accuse him of being "a preacher of foreign deities"—Jesus and a divine female consort, Anastasia (the Greek word translated *resurrection*)—although he only proclaims one God, Jesus, who was raised from the dead (v. 18). These supposed "foreign deities" sound so "strange" to them that, out of curiosity, they invite Paul to explain to them more fully what he means, as is their custom (vv. 19-21).

As the old adage states, "Christians are in the world, but not of it." While we are in the world, we will learn and acquire knowledge about the world, its beliefs, and its customs. We can, and should, use some of what we learn in order to draw culture-to-Christ analogies for unbelievers who cannot comprehend the Gospel. However, personal evangelists who are consistent with Paul's evangelistic methodology in Athens will demonstrate a knowledgeable expertise on Jesus and the resurrection over the trivial pursuit of secular, pop culture facts. In other words, the practice of biblical evangelism is not primarily about what you know (of this world), it's Whom you know (the resurrected Jesus Christ). Preaching the Gospel is as simple as telling others about Jesus and His resurrection from the dead.

– Matt Queen

Guided Prayer:

- Thank God for Jesus and His resurrection from the dead.
- Ask God to prompt, at opportune times, specific cultural beliefs, traditions, and/or arts that can assist you to explain and/or contextualize the Gospel to secular people who have difficulty understanding it.
- Pray that the Holy Spirit will assist you in having follow-up conversations with unbelievers who have indicated that they would be interested in discussing the Gospel with you again.

DAY 24

ACTS 18:1-11

Main Idea: *The presence of Jesus helps us overcome our fear of evangelizing.*

Can you remember your scariest evangelism encounter? I remember mine as if it were yesterday. In 2012, a Southwestern Seminary student and I evangelized house to house, one block east of the seminary campus on West Fuller Avenue. A man in the second house we visited received Christ as his Savior and Lord! Joy and excitement filled our hearts. However, our joy gave way to fear after we arrived at the seventh house on the street.

A group of men congregated around and in the bed of a truck parked in their driveway. Finding themselves at the end of the workday, they socialized about the day's events. We approached the men, introduced ourselves, and proceeded to tell them we were there to share with them how they could have peace with God through Jesus.

As soon as we announced our intentions, all the men began laughing at us. The fear of ridicule took its effect on us. How could we recover the conversation for Christ? I knew I had to reassert myself, so looking directly into the eyes of the biggest man of the group, I retorted, "Is that funny?" No sooner than the words left my mouth, my eyes looked down as he sat in the truck bed and I made a frightful discovery—a gun on his lap! Fear overcame us.

"Funny?" I asked myself. "You better hope this guy thinks it's funny."

Feigning ignorance and filled with fear, I timidly asked him, pointing to the gun in his lap, "Are you going to shoot me with that?" "No, man," he replied, "this is a BB gun." As my fear gave way to confidence,

I pleaded with him, "Well, 'BB' that gun behind you and let me tell you about Jesus." He disarmed himself of the gun, and I dispensed the Gospel to him.

Doubtless, all believers at some time or another face some fear to evangelize. Before his arrival in Corinth, Paul's preaching of the Gospel is met with persecution and expulsion from Pisidian Antioch (Acts 13:50), mistreatment and the threat of stoning in Iconium (14:5), stoning almost to the point of death in Lystra (14:19), flogging and imprisonment in Philippi (16:22-23), and ridicule in Athens (17:32). No wonder Paul's first written correspondence to the Corinthians states that he came to them "in weakness, in fear, and in much trembling" (1 Corinthians 2:3). To a greater extent than any of us, the apostle experienced his own fears in evangelism.

Paul encounters the first of two specific evangelistic fears upon arriving at Corinth—isolation. Paul comes to Corinth alone (Acts 18:1). While in Macedonia, Thessalonian Jews who oppose the Gospel begin a riot in Berea, forcing Paul to leave immediately by sea for Athens. His abrupt departure temporarily separates him from his close companions, Silas and Timothy (17:13-14), until he is able to send word for them to come to him as soon as possible (17:15). Though fearfully alone and isolated in Corinth, Paul nevertheless evangelizes every Sabbath in the synagogue (18:4). After Silas and Timothy arrive from Macedonia in Corinth (18:5a) with a gift from the Philippian church (2 Corinthians 11:8-9; Philippians 4:15-16), Paul devotes himself to preaching the Word daily (18:5b).

Paul also experiences the evangelistic fear of rejection. The Corinthian Jews oppose, revile, and resist Paul's preaching that Jesus is the Messiah (18:5-6). Rejected once again by his own people, Paul turns to preach the Gospel to the Corinthians (18:6-7, 8b).

Despite the belief and baptism of numerous Corinthians, as well as the leader of the synagogue and his family (18:8), Paul fears preaching the Gospel any further. He seriously considers the possibility of becoming a muted evangelist. In fact, his fear becomes so overwhelming that the

Lord Himself appears to him in a night vision. The Lord says to him, "Don't be afraid, but keep on speaking and don't be silent" (18:9).

On what basis is Paul to continue preaching? He is to keep preaching because Jesus is with him! Jesus assures him, "I am with you, and no one will lay a hand on you to hurt you, because I have many people in this city" (18:10).

When you feel alone either because no one evangelizes with you or because unbelievers reject you and the Gospel you preach, remember the comforting words of the Lord to Paul, "I am with you" (18:10a). The presence of Jesus will help you to overcome your fear of evangelizing; therefore, "Don't be afraid, but keep on speaking and don't be silent" (18:9b).

– Matt Queen

Guided Prayer:

- Thank God for His Spirit, who dwells in you, giving you the assurance that you are never alone, even when you are afraid to evangelize.
- Ask the Holy Spirit to embolden you with confidence to overcome your fear of evangelism.
- Ask the Lord that any fear of man that prevents you from evangelizing will give way to the fear of the Lord by which you can persuade men, women, boys, and girls (2 Corinthians 5:11).

DAY 25

ACTS 19:1-7

Main Idea: *Some unbelievers already have a limited understanding of spiritual matters and are ready and willing for a personal evangelist to lead them to Christ.*

The responsibility to share the message of salvation requires a readiness to meet people where they are in their understanding of Jesus. Paul demonstrates such a readiness when he encounters people who have not yet believed in Jesus as Savior and Lord. The example of his witness in Ephesus provides evangelistic insight for personal evangelists today.

Paul had left Antioch and embarked on his third missionary journey. He traveled through the region of Galatia and Phrygia and arrived in the city of Ephesus (Acts 18:22-23). By the time he reached Ephesus, Apollos had crossed the Aegean Sea to Corinth (19:1). Ephesus was a significant city of the day in commerce, culture, and its cosmopolitan flair. The city and surrounding areas desperately needed the good news about Jesus.

In Ephesus, Paul finds some disciples, about twelve men in all. The word *disciples* is typically applied to Christians in the New Testament, people who have already responded to the message about Jesus in repentance and faith. But the discussion between Paul and these twelve reveals that such is not the case for these men. Paul asks them, "Did you receive the Holy Spirit when you believed?" They reply, "No, we haven't even heard that there is a Holy Spirit" (v. 2).

This reply is a curious one. Paul's follow-up question and their answer to it provides further insight into their incomplete understanding. Paul says, "Into what then were you baptized?" They answer, "Into John's baptism" (v. 3).

John the Baptist was the forerunner of Jesus who prepared the way for the public ministry of Jesus. John baptized with a baptism of repentance and indicated that Jesus would baptize with the Holy Spirit (Luke 3:16). Paul explains this to the disciples, saying, "John baptized with a baptism of repentance, telling the people that they should believe in the one who would come after him, that is, in Jesus" (Acts 19:4). John's baptism was anticipatory, and the baptism of Jesus looks back to His finished work of redemption.

Having been instructed in the baptism of John, these disciples should know of the Holy Spirit. The most likely scenario is that while they know of the Holy Spirit, they have not yet heard that He has come. The transitional nature of Acts presents some unique interpretive challenges. In Acts, the Holy Spirit is said to have come into believers at the time of or after baptism (Acts 8:12-16), by the laying on of hands (Acts 8:17), and even before baptism (Acts 10:44, 47-48). Paul later makes it clear that anyone in the New Testament age without the Holy Spirit is not a Christian (Romans 8:9). The disciples in Ephesus have partial information but are not yet Christians.

Upon hearing Paul's teaching, the disciples are "baptized into the name of the Lord Jesus" (Acts 19:5). They accept the message of salvation and submit themselves for baptism in Jesus' name. The experience of the disciples is accompanied by an ecstatic manifestation when they speak in tongues and prophesy (v. 6). The supernatural work of the Holy Spirit in the lives of these men authenticates the message they have received. Ephesus becomes an important center for the Gentile mission, and these disciples likely become an integral part of the mission to Jews and Gentiles.

Several valuable lessons are evident in Paul's encounter with the disciples at Ephesus. God often works ahead of personal evangelists in laying the preparatory groundwork for the proclamation of the Gospel. The disciples have an incomplete understanding, but we could refer to them as seekers. They are seekers because they have already been sought out by God and are interested in learning more. When people are engaged with the Gospel, they often already have some understanding of the truth. Their understanding might be incomplete or even inaccurate, and it is the role of personal evangelists to discern their spiritual condition to lead them to Jesus.

Diagnostic questions are helpful in witnessing encounters to gain perspective of what people may or may not know. Paul gives the disciples he encounters the benefit of the doubt in asking whether they received the Holy Spirit *when* they believed. Today, personal evangelists could, for example, share their testimony and inquire of the people to whom they are speaking about their own testimony regarding Jesus. The response given could yield important information on whether these people indeed have a relationship with Jesus. We should ask questions carefully so that people are not offended unnecessarily.

Understanding a person's spiritual condition then provides an opportunity for personal evangelists to communicate a clear and compelling message of how to follow Jesus in repentance and faith. Sometimes well-intentioned people with a heart to share the Gospel stop short of clearly communicating the message and compelling people to repent and believe. Paul helps the disciples understand the importance of believing in Jesus. As personal evangelists, we must do the same.

Expect people to respond. The personal evangelist calls for others to have faith in Jesus, all the while believing they will do so. Only God can transform a soul. The ministry of Paul is filled with faith, and he expects people to be ready and willing to respond when he tells them about Jesus. Paul knows what Jesus has done in his life and is certain that others need to know the Good News. We must believe in the power of God to convict, convince, and convert; and we must faithfully share Jesus with others.

– Seth Polk

Guided Prayer:

- Thank God for tilling the soil of people's hearts, preparing them to hear and receive our message.
- Pray that God will grant you wisdom in discerning people's spiritual condition, that you may witness to them effectively, asking the right questions and leading them to the truth.
- Pray that God will lead you to those who already have some understanding of the Gospel and are ready and willing to receive it. Pray that you will be faithful in extending a call, and that they will respond in repentance and faith.

DAY 26

ACTS 19:8-10

Main Idea: *Understanding the role of the message and the messenger will spur on our evangelism in the face of persecution.*

Throughout history, many attempts have been made to remove the offense of the Gospel. Although the Apostle Paul is often regarded as the model of Gospel contextualization in his effort to become all things to all men, Paul is never portrayed in Scripture as one who dilutes the Gospel in order to make it more palatable to his audience.

Consider the consequences Paul suffers for preaching the Gospel. He testifies of imprisonments, beatings, and facing often the danger of death (2 Corinthians 11:23). He continues, "Five times I received the forty lashes minus one from the Jews. Three times I was beaten with rods. Once I received a stoning" (vv. 24-25a). If there is any question about who did these things, Paul names his oppressors as the Jews, Gentiles, and false brethren. In other words, everyone was offended by him. This does not sound like the resume of one who mastered the art being "relevant"!

While I do not disregard the importance of healthy contextualization, Scripture indicates that when the Gospel is preached, varying degrees of persecution will inevitably follow. Even in the case of Ephesus—where he experiences exceptional receptivity—Paul's evangelistic ministry is not immune to persecution. In Acts 19, when Paul comes to Ephesus, he enters the synagogue in order to preach. As a result, he baptizes twelve new disciples (vv. 1-7). Luke summarizes what happens next, saying:

Paul entered the synagogue and spoke boldly over a period of three months, arguing and persuading them about the kingdom of God. But when some became hardened and would not believe, slandering the Way in front of the crowd, he withdrew from them, taking the disciples, and conducted discussions every day in the lecture hall of Tyrannus (vv. 8-9).

After an initially receptive start, Paul experiences the beginnings of persecution. Yet, he continues to evangelize. We must ask: How does Paul persevere in evangelism even when facing persecution?

Paul himself gives insight when addressing the Ephesian elders in Miletus (Acts 20:17-38). Two times Paul gives reason why he does "not avoid proclaiming" the Gospel to the Ephesians. These reasons are applicable to us as well.

First, **Paul understands that the message is profitable**. As Paul recalls his persecution in Ephesus, he reminds the elders of his diligence in evangelism, saying, "You know that I did not avoid proclaiming to you anything that was profitable, ... teaching you publicly and from house to house. I testified to both Jews and Greeks about repentance toward God and faith in our Lord Jesus" (vv. 20-21).

Paul says that he has a profitable message. Of course, he does not have worldly profits in mind. He means that the Gospel is the only means that is *useful* for reconciling sinners to a holy God. Paul knows that the only chance the Ephesians have to be saved is through hearing the Good News preached. So, he cannot shrink back. For the sake of their salvation, he has to evangelize.

No matter what kind of spiritual climate surrounds us, we must not be timid about declaring anything profitable for helping others come to a saving faith in Jesus. Christians are often tempted to omit certain truths of Scripture with hopes of increasing receptivity. But let us not think for a moment that we can help anyone by altering the very revelation given for salvation. Declaring the whole message of repentance toward God and faith in Jesus Christ is the only way we can help sinners find salvation.

Second, **Paul understands that the messenger is provisional**. As God's ambassadors, we must grapple with our own mortality. A day will come when each of us will pass. Then, we will be judged and rewarded. Paul shows that he understands this when he says, "Therefore I declare to you this day that I am innocent of the blood of all of you, because I did not avoid declaring to you the whole plan of God" (vv. 26-27). Paul knows that he faces an impending judgment. This future judgment before the Lord is far more important to him than how men judge him in the present. So, even at the threat of his life, he persists in evangelism.

In the end, brothers and sisters, you and I will be held accountable for the message entrusted to us. The reality of our transience should incite a sense of urgency for proclamation. Any good work done for your own glory will vanish, but what is done for the glory of God will last forever. If judgment came today, how would you be found in regard to your evangelism? Would you be judged as one who cowered before the potential threats of men? Or would you be rewarded as one who did not shrink back? May a healthy fear of God drive us to persevere in faithful evangelism.

Despite the threat of persecution in Ephesus, Paul perseveres in evangelism, aided by a sound understanding of the message and the messenger. Scripture records the result: "This went on for two years, so that all the residents of Asia, both Jews and Greeks, heard the word of the Lord" (19:10). The fruit of Paul's perseverance is a local church planted in Ephesus comprising co-laborers in the Great Commission. Thereby, the Word of God spreads mightily throughout that land.

When you encounter opposition, remember that you have a message profitable for the salvation of sinners, and that your days as the messenger are numbered. Be faithful to declare the Gospel, and I pray that you may see the fruit of evangelism grow through your ministry.

- Ricky Don Wilhelm

Guided Prayer:

- Thank God for gifting us a profitable message by which we can be saved, and thank Him for appointing you as His messenger to share it.
- Repent of any times that you diluted the Gospel message in order to please men rather than God in your evangelism.
- Pray that God will grant you deeper understanding of the profitable message of the Gospel and the provisional nature of your role as an evangelist, and that this will lead to perseverance in your evangelism.

DAY 27

ACTS 19:23-41

Main Idea: *While we should always be willing to risk our lives for the sake of the Gospel, there are times when self-preservation, for the sake of ongoing witness, is the necessary choice.*

The loudest recorded roar of a crowd at a modern sporting event occurred in 2014 at Arrowhead Stadium in Kansas City, Missouri, during a Monday night football game between the New England Patriots and the Kansas City Chiefs. Reaching a level of 142.2 decibels, the average decibel level of an aircraft carrier deck receiving jets, the hometown crowd claimed a spot in the record books as the loudest crowd ever. One has to wonder, upon reading Acts 19, how loud the crowd gathered in the theater at Ephesus must have been as they shouted for two hours, "Great is Artemis of the Ephesians!" (v. 34).

Carved into the hillside at Ephesus, this ancient theater, preserved to the modern day, had enough room to seat 25,000 people, or roughly 10 percent of the population of the city of Ephesus in Paul's time. It was home to sporting events and gladiatorial competitions, as well as compelling theatrical productions. In the narrative of Acts 19, however, the theater at Ephesus serves as the stage for the most famous sermon that was never preached.

It might seem natural to begin an investigation of this incident at the start of verse 23, "About that time there was a major disturbance about the Way," but by doing so, you might miss an important element of the story. We must not overlook the fact that Paul preaches and ministers in Ephesus for two years before this riot takes place (v. 10).

The transformative power of the Gospel begins to take effect immediately after he arrives in Ephesus, and he baptizes the few believers he finds "into the name of the Lord Jesus" (v. 5). The Gospel has the power to transform lives and effect change immediately, as we see in verses 11-20; and as it transforms lives, it eventually begins to transform culture. This is the groundwork for what happens next in Ephesus.

The not-so-small disturbance in Ephesus occurs when Demetrius, a silversmith who creates shrines and idols of Artemis, gathers other tradesmen together and points out to them two things: that their livelihood is dependent on the worship of the goddess Artemis, and that her "magnificence" is in jeopardy of coming "to the verge of ruin" because of Paul's teaching (v. 27). Even though Paul has never spoken a word against Artemis (also known as Diana), Demetrius twists the truth in this way, selfishly cloaking his own fear of losing his business in a concern for the proper worship of Artemis. So, the outrage among the people in Ephesus is rooted in selfishness and exacerbated by false arguments.

Hostility to the Gospel is often not due to the content of the message, but to the consequence of the message. In Ephesus, over the course of Paul's ministry, the consequences of the message have begun to influence the economy of the town, which is rooted in idol worship, and this is what compels the craftsman's guild to raise a ruckus. Demetrius' appeal to pocketbooks and provincial pride ultimately leads to the significant disturbance in Ephesus. Verse 29 says, "The city was filled with confusion, and they rushed all together into the amphitheater."

And now we come to Paul's unpreached sermon. In verse 30, we read that "although Paul wanted to go in before the people, the disciples did not let him." Paul is not unaccustomed to speaking to large crowds, and he no doubt has a strong desire to speak to this gathering of Ephesians. Elsewhere in the book of Acts, we see him masterfully, through the guidance of the Holy Spirit, share the Gospel of Jesus Christ among large gatherings of people who are hostile toward him and his message. At Lystra, he is even stoned to the point that his opponents drag him out of the city, supposing him to be dead (14:19). Paul is not averse to confrontation. So why do the disciples and influencers in Ephesus prohibit him from speaking to the gathered assembly?

Paul knows, as he would later write, that "to live is Christ and to die is gain" (Philippians 1:21), and he is prepared to give his life to make Christ known, even in the theater at Ephesus. Perhaps his friends and the officials in the town fear that he will be killed before even speaking a word. It is evident from this narrative that sometimes a spiritual climate is so hostile that preaching may not be possible. While there are times when Christians are called to risk their lives for the sake of sharing the Gospel (like Stephen in Acts 7, or Jim Elliot and his missionary colleagues in Ecuador), there are also times when self-preservation, for the sake of an ongoing witness, is a prudent answer. There is also great wisdom in accountability, much like Paul's companions and the officials provide (Proverbs 11:14; 15:22).

The fact that Paul does not have an opportunity to address the crowd in Ephesus by no means indicates that he is unfaithful to his calling. The church in Ephesus continues to thrive and flourish even after he departs, to the point that it becomes the recipient of one of Paul's letters and one of the seven churches recognized in the book of Revelation. He is consistent, obedient, and faithful day in and day out over the course of two years of ministry in Ephesus. And after being seized two chapters later, Paul continues to faithfully proclaim the Gospel of Jesus Christ as a prisoner.

Brothers and sisters, take heart in Paul's example in Acts 19. There may be occasions when you have a strong desire to share the Gospel, but open hostility toward the message may prohibit you from speaking. But consider the fact that your inability to share in that moment may serve the purpose of preserving you for an ongoing witness at another time. Paul listens to wise counsel around him, and after this encounter, the Holy Spirit leads him to Jerusalem and, ultimately, to Rome to share about the Good News of Jesus Christ. So, keep this in mind: One day, you, too, may have your own unpreached sermon, but rather than dwell on what remains unsaid, take confidence that God may very well have preserved you to be His witness at a later date and in another place.

– Adam Covington

Guided Prayer:

- Thank God for preserving you for the sake of your ongoing witness.
- Ask God for wisdom and guidance regarding when you should put your life at risk in order to share the Gospel, and when you should seek self-preservation in order to share the Gospel at another time.
- Pray that you will be found faithful regardless of what God calls you to do—whether to face death by sharing the Gospel in a dangerous situation, or to follow His lead to evangelize at a later date in another place.

DAY 28

ACTS 21:27-22:22

Main Idea: *As Christians, we will face persecution; but this can further, rather than hinder, our evangelism.*

The persecution and violent opposition of the world to the followers of Christ have been living realities for the saints of God throughout the ages. Jesus says to His disciples in John 15:20, "Remember the word I spoke to you: 'A servant is not greater than his master.' If they persecuted me, they will also persecute you. If they kept my word, they will also keep yours." Jesus taught His disciples that they would experience persecution. He called them to consider the cost of discipleship before deciding to follow Him. In Matthew 16:24-25, we read, "Then Jesus said to his disciples, 'If anyone wants to follow after me, let him deny himself, take up his cross, and follow me. For whoever wants to save his life will lose it, but whoever loses his life because of me will find it.'"

Furthermore, Paul says in 2 Timothy 3:12, "In fact, all who want to live a godly life in Christ Jesus will be persecuted." Paul even refers to suffering for Christ as a gift from God. He says in Philippians 1:29-30, "For it has been granted to you on Christ's behalf not only to believe in him, but also to suffer for him, since you are engaged in the same struggle that you saw I had and now hear that I have." As we receive this free gift of salvation and follow Christ, know that discipleship will be costly.

The world will persecute Christians for their faith in Christ, but such persecution also provides an opportunity for Christian witness. God often allows suffering for Christ in order that the saints of God may have opportunities to share the Gospel. In Luke 21:12-13, Jesus says to

His disciples, "But before all these things, they will lay their hands on you and persecute you. They will hand you over to the synagogues and prisons, and you will be brought before kings and governors because of my name. This will give you an opportunity to bear witness."

The Apostle Paul knows what it means to be imprisoned, rejected by his own people, and violently attacked for the sake of the Gospel. In Acts 21:27-22:22, Luke records the account of Paul's testimony of Christ in Jerusalem, the violent response of the Jewish people, and the beginning of Paul's Roman imprisonment. From a human point of view, Paul's experience seems like a tragedy; but from God's point of view, Paul's suffering is ordained for the spread of the Gospel.

Paul is compelled to go to Jerusalem and share Christ with his own countrymen, despite repeated warnings from his fellow Christians not to go (21:10-12). After Paul is falsely accused of bringing uncircumcised Gentiles into the temple, Jewish leaders stir the crowd in Jerusalem to kill Paul. God intervenes by sending Roman troops to rescue Paul from certain death. Paul asks and receives from the Roman commander an opportunity to speak to the Jewish crowd. He takes the opportunity to share in Hebrew his personal testimony of conversion to Christ.

People listen intently until he speaks of being called to take the message of salvation to the Gentiles. The crowd reacts violently, seeking to kill Paul, and when that fails, they try to entrap him in the Jewish religious court. As a Roman citizen, Paul is able to appeal to Caesar and avoid a sham trial in Jerusalem.

On his way to Rome to stand before Caesar, Paul shares Christ in his imprisonment before Roman leaders, soldiers, and all with whom he comes into contact. The book of Acts ends with Paul sharing Christ in prison. God ordained Paul's suffering as a means of extending the Gospel to a lost world.

God calls all of His people to share Christ with others, bearing testimony to the transformation that Christ has accomplished in their lives. The response of unbelievers to our testimony will always be mixed; some will receive Christ as Lord and Savior, but many will reject Him.

Increasingly around the world today, Christian testimony is met with violent opposition and persecution. Christians should not be surprised at this response. Followers of Christ represent the light of Christ in a dark world, and because people love darkness rather than light, the world will reject the Christian message. We know from Paul's experience, and that of the saints throughout the ages, that such violent encounters often lead to the spread of the Gospel.

Christ reminds us that as the world treated Him, so it will treat His people. We must take heart, because He has overcome the world. Though we will be opposed, maligned, and attacked in this world for the sake of the Gospel, Christ has promised to empower us for witness, to grow His church, and to be with us until the end of the age. He calls us to steadfastness because His Kingdom is at hand. Satan is at work opposing Christian witness at every turn, but greater is He who is in us than he who is in the world. The Apostle John reminds us in Revelation 12:11, "They conquered him by the blood of the Lamb and by the word of their testimony; for they did not love their lives to the point of death." May the love of Christ so constrain us to share Him with others that we love not our lives unto death.

– John D. Massey

Guided Prayer:

- Thank God for filling you with the Holy Spirit to empower you to bear witness to Christ with unbelievers.
- Ask God to give you Spirit-empowered courage to be faithful to Christ in the face of opposition from unbelieving friends and family.
- Pray that God will strengthen your faith to know that He is with you at all times and has overcome death and the devil.

ACTS 24:24-27

Main Idea: *Gospel opposition often leads to Gospel opportunities.*

Bill Wallace (1908-1951) served as a Southern Baptist medical missionary for fifteen years, working as a surgeon at Stout Memorial Hospital in Wuchow, China. He was beloved by all who knew him and worked tirelessly to save as many lives as possible, all while sharing the Gospel that could save their souls from eternal death. In 1950, Wallace was arrested under the suspicion of acting as a spy and was subjected to brutal interrogations, beatings, and ridicule. This treatment went on for several months, yet Wallace continued sharing the Gospel in the midst of opposition.

In Acts 24, Paul faces a similar experience in which he is on trial before Felix, Roman governor of Judea. At this point in his life, Paul has experienced much tribulation for Christ: arrested multiple times, beaten, mocked, and nearly stoned to death. Yet, in the midst of these trials, Paul faithfully shares the Gospel as the occasion arises. In fact, some might even say that the opposition he faces opens the door for multiple Gospel opportunities. Standing before Felix and those who bring charges against him, Paul gives a defense of his ministry and a clear Gospel proclamation (vv. 10-21). Though these facts seem to clear Paul's name from any accusations, Felix delays the trial and gives orders for Paul to remain in custody (vv. 22-23).

Shortly after his detainment, Paul is summoned once again by Felix, this time privately, with only his wife, Drusilla, present. Paul finds himself standing before one of the most powerful men in the world—a man who has the power to sentence him to death or to set him free. In this moment, Paul is faced with a choice. He can bargain his way out of his current bondage, or he can stand firm in his commitment to preach Christ in the midst of opposition. This opposition to the Gospel creates an opportunity for Paul to proclaim the Gospel in four specific ways.

First, Paul makes a choice to proclaim the Gospel **boldly**. He understands the possible ramifications of such a choice more than most. As mentioned above, Paul has experienced persecution for the Gospel, and much of this was brought on because of his choice to boldly speak of Christ in the face of opposition. However, Paul also understands the reality that "to live is Christ and to die is gain" (Philippians 1:21), which gives him the ability to stand firm against Gospel opposition and speak the Gospel boldly.

Second, Paul makes a choice to proclaim the Gospel **directly**. Often when facing opposition, we are tempted to speak lightly or around a controversial issue. Knowing that the Gospel is the reason he is in prison, Paul is aware that if he continues speaking about Jesus, the result will not be pleasant for him personally. However, when summoned by Felix and Drusilla, Paul chooses to speak "on the subject of faith in Christ Jesus" (v. 24) instead of watering down the Gospel. Paul understands that faith in Christ alone is the central point of the Gospel and that he must speak directly on the matter, so that there is no confusion or lack of clarity toward the Gospel and its implications.

Third, Paul makes a choice to proclaim the Gospel **personally**. Throughout his ministry, Paul presents the Gospel with a keen awareness of the audience he is addressing at the time. In Acts 17, Paul addresses the crowds at the Areopagus as "extremely religious in every respect," makes reference to the altar to the unknown god, and then addresses the fact that they have missed the risen Savior, Jesus Christ (vv. 22-31). In Acts 24, Paul understands that Felix is a judge of civil matters and that he will understand the concept of judgment. Therefore, Paul discusses righteousness, self-control, and the judgment to come, which effectively brings a state of fear over Felix to the point that he dismisses Paul from his presence (v. 25). Paul knows not only how to proclaim the

Gospel generally; he knows how to proclaim the Gospel specifically to individuals so that the message resonates in the hearts of his audience.

Finally, Paul makes a choice to proclaim the Gospel **continually**. When one experiences Gospel opposition, the natural tendency is to walk away and never return. The unpleasant experience of rejection or persecution can discourage the believer from making further attempts at proclaiming the Gospel. However, Paul does not allow such discouraging moments to hinder Gospel advancement. Instead, Paul takes advantage of these opportunities and even is able to make multiple contacts with Felix over the next few years until Felix is succeeded by Porcius Festus (vv. 26-27).

Bill Wallace died on February 10, 1951, after being brutally tortured and tormented for several months. In facing such persecution, Wallace could have chosen to end this treatment by giving in to his persecutors. Instead, he chose to stay the course and accept any consequences that would come. Christians must choose to proclaim the Gospel boldly, directly, personally, and continually in the face of Gospel opposition. Though physical persecution is not as prevalent in today's society, there may come a day when this changes. Before this happens, Christians must make a choice to not let Gospel opposition hinder Gospel advancement.

– Brandon Kiesling

Guided Prayer:

- Thank God for granting us the privilege of bearing His name and suffering for His sake (Philippians 1:29; Acts 5:41).
- Pray that God will open your eyes to see the Gospel opportunities brought about by Gospel opposition.
- Ask that God will sustain you in the face of persecution, that you may proclaim the Gospel boldly, directly, personally, and continually.

DAY 30

ACTS 25:23-26:32

Main Idea: *Every interaction can be redeemed as an evangelistic opportunity.*

After being violently seized by the Jews in Jerusalem, Paul was arrested, flogged, beaten, and imprisoned for several years. He testified before the Jews in the temple, he testified before the Sanhedrin, he testified before Felix, and he testified before Festus. Now we find a climax of sorts for Paul's journey through the Judean court system, as he testifies finally before Agrippa, king of Judea.

Officially, Paul's testimony is to be a defense against his accusers. Unofficially, however, Paul clearly has another objective in mind.

After discreetly providing an apologetic defense for his ministry by rooting it in the Old Testament promises of God (Acts 26:6-8), Paul shares his testimony of how he came to know the Lord. He objectively relates what Jesus said to him on the road to Damascus that day—"I am sending you ... to open [Jews' and Gentiles'] eyes so that they may turn from darkness to light and from the power of Satan to God, that they may receive forgiveness of sins and a share among those who are sanctified by faith in me" (vv. 17b-18). Don't miss what Paul is doing here. Under the guise of relating Jesus' words to him on the road to Damascus, he is explaining to the court that his ministry has aimed to turn people from darkness to light, from Satan to God, from sin and death to forgiveness and eternal life. And such salvation, he says, can be experienced through faith in Jesus. In short, Paul is presenting the Gospel.

Paul continues that he was obedient to this charge from the Lord, faithfully preaching that people should repent from their sins, turn to God, and prove their repentance through their deeds. (Note again Paul's explanation of the Gospel via his objective reporting of his ministry.) For this reason, Paul says, the Jews seized him and tried to put him to death, and this is why he stands on trial before Agrippa today.

Paul concludes with his third and most explicit articulation of the Gospel (though once again presented objectively as the message he has been preaching). He states, "To this very day, I have had help from God, and I stand and testify to both small and great, saying nothing other than what the prophets and Moses said would take place—that the Messiah must suffer, and that, as the first to rise from the dead, he would proclaim light to our people and to the Gentiles" (vv. 22-23).

Several things are clear from Paul's statements:

1. Christ died according to the Scriptures and was resurrected from the dead.
2. Salvation comes by faith in this resurrected Christ.
3. This salvation is available to all, Jew and Gentile alike.
4. Among the fruit of salvation is visible repentance from sin and submission and obedience to the Lord.
5. Those who believe in Jesus are saved from darkness and the dominion of Satan.
6. Those who believe in Jesus will receive an inheritance among those who have been sanctified by faith in Him.

Consider something interesting about the fact that Paul has managed to communicate this many components of the Gospel: Paul is not preaching in a church; he is not freely evangelizing on a street corner or in the marketplace; he has not been invited to explicitly preach by fellow believers, curious seekers, or even enemies aiming to trap him by his words; he is testifying in open court before pagan officials as a defense against his accusers. And yet Paul has managed to clearly and thoroughly communicate the Good News of Jesus Christ. He has redeemed this interaction with King Agrippa and the rest of his audience as an evangelistic opportunity.

Though Paul's method is subtle ("I'm merely explaining what I have preached before," he might say), Agrippa eventually discerns Paul's aim. After Festus accuses Paul of being out of his mind (for why else would Paul not defend himself but rather proclaim the very message that got him in trouble to begin with?), Paul appeals directly to Agrippa and the king's knowledge of the prophets, whom Paul has already said testified to Jesus' death and resurrection. Not to be fooled by Paul's unashamed ulterior motive, Agrippa replies, "Are you going to persuade me to become a Christian so easily?" (v. 28).

His true purpose revealed, Paul abandons all subtlety and boldly declares, "I wish before God that whether easily or with difficulty, not only you but all who listen to me today might become as I am—except for these chains" (v. 29).

What seemingly began as a simple recounting of events ends as a full-fledged Gospel presentation, complete with an invitation to believe by faith. Paul utilizes this opportunity not to defend himself, be cleared of charges, and be set free; instead, he redeems this interaction with Agrippa, Festus, his immediate audience, and the listening world as an opportunity for evangelism.

What an amazing example of faithful evangelistic witness! In the midst of such grievous circumstances, Paul still maintains his focus on the Gospel and utilizes this opportunity to share the Good News of Christ with an audience to whom he likely would not have been able to witness otherwise. They hear the message of salvation because he redeems the situation for their good and God's glory.

Brothers and sisters, may we follow Paul's example. We will find ourselves in a multitude of different scenarios throughout our lives, some of them negative, like Paul (e.g., wrongful imprisonment due to religious persecution, court testimony before unsympathetic officials), and some of them more neutral (e.g., sitting in a restaurant, walking through a park, etc.). In every scenario, we will find opportunities to interact with individuals who may be lost, hurting, and in need of the light of the Gospel. No matter what the circumstances, all of these interactions can be redeemed as evangelistic opportunities.

We can share the Gospel with the person walking past us in the park or the server who is waiting our table. We can share the Gospel with fellow inmates in prison or the officials hearing our testimony in court. All of these situations can be open doors to sharing the Gospel.

And our methodology can be subtle, like Paul's. We do not always have to open with, "If you were to die today and stand at the gate of heaven, and God were to ask you why He should let you in, what would you say?" There is a time to ask this question, but in some situations, perhaps we can simply start a friendly conversation. And as we and those to whom we speak share about what is important to us, we can mention that the most important thing about us is our relationship with Jesus Christ. From there, we can share our testimony of how we came to know the Lord. In so doing, we can share the Gospel. And after sharing the Gospel, then we can say something like, "What do you think about that? Do you have a relationship with Jesus? Would you like to?"

So as we go about our everyday lives, let us remember Paul's example. He could have had other things on his mind as he testified before Agrippa, but instead, he maintained a Gospel focus, and so he redeemed this very unique interaction as an opportunity for evangelism. As we interact with others throughout our day-to-day lives, may we, in like manner, utilize every encounter as an evangelistic opportunity, sharing our stories so that the lost may hear the Gospel and believe and be saved.

– Alex Sibley

Guided Prayer:

- Thank God for providing you opportunities to proclaim your story of His greatness so that the lost may hear and be saved.

- Pray that God will help you maintain a Gospel focus and utilize every interaction for Gospel proclamation.
- Pray for wisdom in how to share your story, that those who hear it might come to know the Lord.

DAY 31

ACTS 28:17-31

Main Idea: *We must continue sharing the Gospel as long as God gives us opportunities to do so.*

Do you ever get tired? Of course, we all do, but in the context of ministry, do you ever grow weary in the evangelistic task? Do you ever think to yourself, "I might go out and evangelize to my neighbors if only I weren't so tired," or, "I know I should share the Gospel with my server at this restaurant, but I'm just too tired"? Or perhaps, in a "big picture" sense, "I have been evangelizing for many years now; I think I've earned an extended break"?

By the end of the book of Acts, Paul is likely very tired. He has ministered for many years, and this in itself is exhausting work. But in addition to that, he has also endured much hardship, persecution, suffering, illness, violent assaults, multiple imprisonments, a treacherous sea voyage, and a traumatic shipwreck. If faced with similar circumstances, we would likely be tempted to retire from ministry altogether due to sheer exhaustion.

And yet Paul perseveres.

Following his bold testimony before King Agrippa, the king affirms that Paul could have been set free, but because Paul appealed to Caesar, he has to be sent to Rome (Acts 25:11; 26:32). Though he first has to endure a storm and a shipwreck and even a bite from a venomous snake, here at the end of the book of Acts, Paul has finally arrived at the center of the Roman Empire. And though we would hardly blame him for deciding to take an extended respite from the ministry at this point, Paul remains faithful to the evangelistic task.

Calling together the leaders of the Jews, Paul explains how he became a prisoner in the hands of the Romans. When the Jews reply that they have not heard of this ordeal but that they are curious to know his views on the hope of Israel, Paul testifies to them about the Kingdom of God and tries to persuade them concerning Jesus from both the Law and the Prophets (28:21-23). Though some are persuaded, others do not believe. Nevertheless, for the next two years, Paul continues preaching the Kingdom and teaching about Jesus "with all boldness and without hindrance" (v. 31).

While good stewardship of our bodies certainly allows for seeking rest from time to time, whenever we feel too exhausted to share the Gospel, despite having the opportunity to do so, we would do well to remember Paul's example. He does not make excuses. When God gives him the opportunity to share the Gospel, he does so. And God gives him many opportunities.

Though Paul comes to Rome in chains, God provides him opportunities to evangelize from his home (vv. 17, 30). And when Paul preaches to the Jews about Jesus and the Kingdom of God, many disagree with him and begin to leave (v. 25); and yet God continues to provide him opportunities to evangelize (v. 30). In fact, Paul stays for two whole years and apparently never stops proclaiming the Gospel of Jesus Christ. God keeps giving him opportunities to evangelize, and so Paul keeps on evangelizing.

Paul writes in his letter to the Galatians that we must not get tired of doing good, for at the proper time, we will reap a harvest if we do not give up (Galatians 6:9). These clearly are not empty words to Paul; he lives them out. He perseveres in the task and keeps preaching as long as God keeps giving him opportunities to do so. As Paul himself exhorts, we must do likewise. If God gives us the opportunity to evangelize, we must not make excuses; we must be faithful to the task.

But this Scripture points to an even greater point, as well. It is interesting that the book of Acts ends here, with Paul preaching from "his own rented house" in Rome. Though preceding chapters depict Paul's progressive journey to Rome to ultimately testify before Caesar, the book ends before we see this testimony delivered. Multiple possible explanations exist for why this is so (for example, perhaps Acts was written before Paul testified). But a deeper meaning may be found in the open-ended nature of the book's conclusion. After all, this Scripture is inspired by God Himself (2 Timothy 3:16), and He surely had reason to end the book where He did. Though the book does not climax with Paul's testimony before Caesar as modern readers might expect, its open-endedness highlights an important point for us as personal evangelists. Specifically, it highlights the ongoing nature of the evangelistic task.

In other words, not only is it imperative that we not grow weary in the immediate sense, but it is imperative in the big picture sense, as well. That is, we must never give up. The task remains undone, and so we must never stop sharing the Gospel.

The book of Acts opens with Jesus appointing His followers as witnesses for Him to the ends of the earth, and it ends with Paul continually witnessing for Christ from the heart of the Roman Empire, fulfilling that very calling. This thematic unity between beginning and end emphasizes the fact that we must always be about the work of the Lord. He has appointed us for a task, and that task remains undone. We must bring the Gospel to every corner of the world so that all may hear the Good News of salvation through faith in Jesus Christ. Just as Paul kept on preaching, so we must keep on spreading the Gospel as long as God gives us the opportunity to do so.

And if the book of Acts proves anything, it's that God will give His people opportunities to evangelize, that the lost may hear and be saved. So let us not get tired of doing good, but rather let us continually proclaim the Gospel of Jesus Christ. For at the proper time, we *will* reap a harvest *if* we do not give up.

– Alex Sibley

Guided Prayer:

- Thank the Lord for providing opportunities for sinners (including, at one time, you) to hear the Gospel so that they may be reconciled to Him.
- Pray that the Lord will empower you to not become weary in the evangelistic task, but to persevere in spreading the Gospel.
- Pray that God will help you to always be about His work, that all may hear of His Good News, even in the remotest part of the earth.

LAST WORD

Hopefully you have not waited until you finished these devotionals to go out and evangelize. Nevertheless, an obvious "last word" for this book is an exhortation for you to go and share the Gospel. We pray that you have been encouraged by this guided study of the Word of God, and now we pray that you go out and seek to accomplish the task. Share the Gospel with the lost, that they may hear and be saved. We wholeheartedly believe that God will bless your efforts, and eternity will be impacted as a result.

As you contemplate the things discussed in this book, consider finally Jesus' words in the Great Commission of Matthew 28:

> All authority has been given to me in heaven and on earth. Go, therefore, and make disciples of all nations, baptizing them in the name of the Father and of the Son and of the Holy Spirit, teaching them to observe everything I have commanded you. And remember, I am with you always, to the end of the age (vv. 18b-20).

The One who possesses all authority in heaven and on earth has commanded us to bring His Gospel to the nations. The King of the universe has given us this specific charge. May we be found obedient.

May we also be comforted that He who reigns over all creation has promised to be with us even to the end of the age. Indeed, as He said in Acts 1:8, we will be empowered for the task by His Spirit, who literally dwells within us. So may we be obedient to our great King, and may we also be overwhelmingly comforted that this same King will go with us as we embark upon this great mission.

So, brothers and sisters, as those who have been appointed witnesses for Christ, go! Proclaim the Gospel. Make disciples. Persevere until the whole world knows that *Jesus saves!*

Additional resources
from Seminary Hill Press

Everyday Evangelism by **Matt Queen**
Encouragement, insight, and practical steps
for creating a culture of everyday evangelism
in your church.

Mobilize to Evangelize by **Matt Queen**
Helpful tools to understand/assess how
evangelism is conceived, practiced, and
perceived in one's congregation, along with
realistic ideas for championing evangelism in
the church.

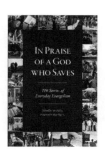

*In Praise of a God who Saves: 110 Stories of
Everyday Evangelism* **edited by Alex Sibley**
110 individual testimonies of God's saving
grace through the evangelism efforts of
SWBTS students, faculty, and staff.

Satisfied? by **Matt Queen**
A Gospel tract that uses the topic of
satisfaction to lead the lost to Christ.

For more information on these and other titles,
visit SeminaryHillPress.com